From Quartermaster to Postmaster to Prompt Master

How a Life of Service Became a Blueprint for the AI Era

Kim A.A. Willis

Kidovi Holdings LLC

Marietta, Georgia

Published by Kidovi Holdings LLC

Marietta, Georgia

ISBN: 979-8-9957889-1-1

First Edition, 2026

kidoviai.com

kidoviholdings.com

thekimwillis.com

Printed in the United States of America

First published 2026

For Dominic and Victoria.

KI. DO. VI.

You are the reason I build anything at all.

For Keary, Gloria, and Tina.

My siblings. My witnesses. My people.

You were there for all of it.

In memory of those who are no longer here to turn these pages,

but whose presence lives in every word:

Troy Anthony Willis

July 10, 1969 – October 23, 1975

Gone too soon. Never forgotten.

Ernest Preston Willis

April 3, 1947 – October 12, 1985

You did not get to hold him. You taught me to hold on anyway.

Donna Elizabeth Willis

March 28, 1947 – June 28, 1998

Peaceful smile. Broken but never defeated. You are on every page.

Hebrew Thompson (Dad) and Gloria Thompson (Mom)

You held a front row seat to everything until death parted you both.

Annie Mae Willis (Grandmom) and John Willis (Grandpop)

Loved, remembered, and honored always.

And for my father, one more time.

You built a purple motorcycle in our basement from scratch.

I am still building.

I learned it and so much more from you.

K I M.

Keep It Moving.

This is not a slogan. It is not a hashtag. It is not a brand device.

It is the instruction I have given myself every time the machine jammed,

every time the door closed, every time the path I expected

became the path I did not.

It is my name.

It is my mantra.

It is my credo.

It is the only strategy that has never failed me.

When you do not know what to do next:

KIM.

Keep It Moving.

Acknowledgments

I could not write thirty-eight years and not stop to acknowledge the people who lived them with me.

To my postal family, across four states and more stations than I can count, Pennsylvania, Georgia, Florida, and California: thank you. The memories we built together, the long shifts, the difficult days, the moments of genuine joy in the middle of work that was harder than it looked from the outside, I carry all of it. We worked alongside each other in ways that no job description ever fully captured. Many of you I still count as friends today. We may not talk as often as we once did, but you are on my mind regularly, and I hope and pray that all is well with you and yours.

To the men and women I served with in the United States Navy: you shaped me in ways I am still discovering. It started in Boot Camp, where a group of women were dropped into the same pressure, the same exhaustion, the same everything, and came out the other side as something closer than friends. Those women became sisters. Not coworkers. Not colleagues. Sisters. You know who you are and you know what that bond means. It does not expire. It does not require proximity to remain real. And to my shipmates at my first and only command, the people I served alongside day in and day out once the real work began: I carry those memories too. I am grateful for every one of you.

To my fellow trainers in healthcare IT, the colleagues who shared classrooms and go-live floors with me across facilities and time zones: you are who I mean when I say the work was good. We showed up together, stayed late together, and made sure the people in front of us had what they needed to do their jobs. That kind of partnership does not go unnoticed or unappreciated. Many of you I still consider friends, and I am glad our paths crossed the way they did. And to the physicians, nurses, technicians, and every member of the clinical and administrative staff I had the privilege of training over the years: if you are reading this, I hope the systems we worked through together are still serving you well, and I hope your work continues to be the meaningful, demanding, necessary thing that it is. You were never just a training room. You were the reason the work mattered.

And to the community I am building in the AI era, the colleagues, collaborators, and fellow builders I have already met and those I have not yet had the pleasure of knowing: I look forward to what we are going to create together. This space is big enough for all of us, and I am glad we are in it at the same time.

And to Alicia Lyttle, whose AI Business Power Circle and Certified AI Consultant program changed the trajectory of what I thought was possible in this season of my life. Alicia is not just a mentor. She is a community leader, a nurturer, an innovator, and one of the most genuinely invested forces in the AI space I have ever encountered. She pours into her community with the kind of consistency and intention that most people only talk about. Her belief that no one gets left behind in the AI revolution is not a slogan. It is how she shows up every single day. This book exists, in part, because of the room she built and the standard she set inside it.

To all of you: this book exists because of the life we shared. Thank you for being part of it.

KIM. Keep It Moving.

Contents

Acknowledgments 7
A Note to the Reader 13
Introduction: The Three Hats 17
Chapter One: The Fire 23
Chapter Two: The Quartermaster 45
Chapter Three: The Headaches 65
Chapter Four: The Long Way Home 81
Chapter Five: The Mastery 99
Chapter Six: The Postmaster 115
Chapter Seven: The Healthcare Years 133
Chapter Eight: The Prompt Master 149
Chapter Nine: The Next Level 163
Chapter Ten: The Blueprint 177
Chapter Eleven: The Stack 191
Chapter Twelve: The Next Navigator 203
Photo Gallery 215
About the Author 239
Work with Kidovi AI 242
The Prompt Master Toolkit 245

A Note to the Reader

This book is a memoir. It is also a manual.

The memoir part is mine. The names, the dates, the places, the people. The house on W. Willard Street. The automation floor at 30th and Market. The zodiac on the range. The U-Haul on the highway. The porch. The certificate. The gold cartouche. All of it happened. All of it is true to the best of my knowledge and recollection, and where my memory has been uncertain I have gone back to records, to family, to the evidence of a life that left paper trails even when I was not thinking about leaving them.

A note on one of those paper trails: the Inquirer article about the fire that took my brother Troy on October 23, 1975 reported that my grandfather walked twenty blocks to a bus stop that morning. The family knows that is not accurate. He walked to the corner. 20th and Willard Streets. Steps from the front door. I have included the article as it was printed and corrected the record alongside it. That is my right as a family historian and as the granddaughter of Hebrew Thompson.

The manual part is for you. The practical chapters in this book, the sections on AI tools and systems and how to begin, are not hypothetical. They reflect how I actually work and what I actually teach. The tools I mention are real. The prompts I describe are ones I use. If something in these pages makes you want to try something, try it. That is the point.

A few names have been withheld by choice. Some people who made my life difficult do not deserve the real estate. Some client relationships are still in progress and belong to a later chapter. I have been transparent about these omissions where they occur.

One item referenced in this book has been confirmed through the USPS Postmaster Finder: I am the first African American woman to serve as Postmaster of Thomson, Georgia, and the 8th officially appointed Postmaster in that Post Office's history. The record is established.

Everything else you are about to read is the truth as I have lived it and as I carry it.

Thank you for picking up this book. I wrote it for the person who needed to know that the machine jamming was not the end of the story.

It was just the beginning of the next one.

Kim A.A. Willis

Marietta, Georgia, 2026

Introduction: The Three Hats

There is a photograph I keep.

My grandfather, Hebrew Thompson, is sitting in his chair on the porch of 1933 W. Willard Street in North Philadelphia. On his head is my NOSC ball cap, the one I wore when I served at Naval Ocean Systems Center Point Loma in San Diego, California. My grandmother Gloria is sitting on the arm of the same chair, leaning into him the way she always leaned into him, the way you lean into someone when decades of doing it has made it as natural as breathing. He is wearing my hat. She is wearing her smile. They are together, the way they were always together, until they were not.

I look at that photograph and I see three things at once.

I see a single mother from North Philadelphia who put on a uniform at twenty-two years old and went looking for the world. I see a woman who came home from that world and resumed spending thirty-eight years building something inside an institution that did not always deserve her. And I see the person she is becoming now, at fifty-eight, at the beginning of the chapter that might be the most important one she has ever started.

Three hats. Three careers. One through line.

The first hat was not the Navy one. It was the postal one, and I want to be honest about that because the order matters.

I started at the United States Postal Service in January 1986 as a casual clerk making five dollars an hour, with a newborn son, a biology textbook I no longer had time to open, and the quiet understanding that the forensic pathologist dream was going into a drawer for a while. I did not know then that I would spend thirty-eight years inside that institution. I did not know I would rise from a casual clerk to a Postmaster. I just knew I needed to work and my mother was not going to let me stop.

The Quartermaster hat came next. I enlisted in the United States Navy on September 28, 1989, at the MEPS, the Military Entrance Processing Station, at Broad and Cherry Street in Philadelphia, with my son Dominic, his father Greg, and my mother Donna Willis standing beside me. I raised my right hand, took an oath and meant every word. I served. I went in as an E-1 and left as an E-4. I had actually tested and successfully passed my E-5 but was discharged before the promotion. I accomplished this within a span of 22 months. I was discharged in July 1991 with an honorable discharge on medical grounds, a scar on my right knee, migraines that have never fully left, and a disability rating that took years of fighting to get right. I am a 100% disabled veteran. I am proud of that service and I am honest about what it cost.

The Postmaster hat completed a Postal Service career that began in January 1986 as a casual clerk and moved to the automation floor by September of that same year. I came back from California, went back to the Post Office, and spent the next three decades climbing from that automation floor to a Postmaster's position with a certificate signed by the first and only female Postmaster General of the United States. In between those two moments were promotions and attempted wrongful removals and lump sum settlements and union grievances and holiday T-shirts and personalized awards and the kind of sustained, daily excellence that does not make headlines but keeps an institution running.

The Prompt Master hat is the newest one. It does not have a uniform or a certificate from a centuries-old institution behind it. What it has is a gold Egyptian cartouche around my neck with my family's name spelled out in hieroglyphics, a certification from the International Association of AI Consultants, a website at kidoviai.com, and the same instinct that has driven every chapter of this life: find the system, learn it completely, make it work for people who need it, and do not stop until the work is done.

This book is the story of how those three hats fit together. How a girl from a block in North Philadelphia who wanted to be a forensic pathologist and became a postal worker who became a sailor who became a Postmaster who became an EMR trainer who became an AI consultant never actually changed who she was. She just kept learning new languages for the same essential thing she has always been doing.

The machine jams. The horizon closes. The medication changes you. The institution tries to stop you. The manager is afraid of your potential. None of it is the end.

It is just the beginning of the next chapter.

Welcome to mine.

Kim A.A. Willis

The Fire

The street was called Willard.

Blocks of rowhouses in North Philadelphia, the kind of street where everybody knew everybody, where the kids ran and played in the streets all day, where the smell of somebody's dinner was always in the air. Our house was at 1925 W. Willard. My grandparents, Gloria and Hebrew Thompson's house was at 1933, four doors away on the same block. Close enough to holler across the porches. Close enough to borrow sugar. Close enough that on a morning in October 1975, my mother could hear the commotion before she even looked out the window.

I was eight years old. My brother Troy was six.

Troy Anthony Willis had been born July 10, 1969, two years after me, the second child of Ernest and Donna Willis, the first son, the one who had my father's last name and my mother's eyes and everybody's heart. He had asthma. That's the detail that doesn't leave you. Not some dramatic thing. Not some rare condition. Asthma. A six-year-old boy with asthma, asleep upstairs in his grandparents' house on the morning of October 23rd in 1975 while Hebrew, lovingly referred to as Dad, stepped to the corner of Willard and 20th Street to help my aunt Donnetta catch her wheelchair-accessible school bus.

I need to tell you about Donnetta for a moment, because she matters to this story. Donnetta was my grandparents' daughter, my mother's sister, my aunt. She was also nearly 9 months older than me. My grandmother Gloria and my mother had been pregnant at nearly the same time, barely a month apart, the kind of overlap that happens in close families where generations run together. Donnetta had been born with disabilities that confined her to a wheelchair most of her life. She needed a specialized wheelchair-accessible bus to get to school. My grandparents' home was her home. Gloria and Hebrew Thompson had been together and would remain together until death parted them. That morning, Dad walked Donnetta to the corner so she could board her bus, the same as he did every school day.

That is what he was doing on the morning of October 23rd in 1975. He stepped to the corner of 20th and Willard Streets, not twenty blocks, not even twenty yards from their front door, to put Donnetta on her bus. He was gone minutes. When he returned, the lower floor of his family's home was already in flames.

Nobody knows exactly how it started. By the time it was reported, the lower half of the house was already burning. My grandfather returned from the corner to find his family's home in flames. He tried to get inside to reach Troy. He could not.

My mother ran from our house.

> ***Donna Willis, 26 years old, attempted to scale a burning building to get to her son.***

I was standing on the Garretts' sidewalk, directly across the street, watching. That image has never left me, an eight-year-old girl rooted to that spot, unable to move, watching my grandparents' house fill with smoke, and not yet understanding the gravity of the entire situation. I remember watching first responders grabbing my mother. Trying to hold her back as she moved toward the fire. She kept going. She was going to climb the walls of that house if she had to. A mother's body doesn't recognize impossibility when her child is inside. She was driven back by the flames and the heavy smoke, the same as my grandfather. The firemen arrived and had the blaze out in twenty-one minutes.

Twenty-one minutes.

Troy was found in the second-floor rear bedroom. He was pronounced dead at Temple University Hospital.

He was six years old.

THE PHILADELPHIA INQUIRER

By ROBERT J. TERRY | Inquirer Staff Writer

A 6-year-old boy suffering from asthma was asphyxiated and five members of another family were injured, two of them critically, in separate house fires yesterday.

The boy, Troy Willis, of 1925 W. Willard died when fire wrecked the first floor of his grandfather's home at 1933 W. Willard shortly before 10 a.m. Police said Troy's grandfather, Hebrew Thompson, 59, left the boy playing in the living room of his home while he took his daughter, Donita, to a bus stop about 20 blocks away. When he returned, he found the lower half of his home in flames. Police said Thompson tried unsuccessfully to enter the house to reach his grandson.

Troy's mother, Donna, 26, ran from her home to try to help but she, too, was driven back by flames and heavy smoke. Firemen arrived and put out the blaze in 21 minutes. The boy was found in a second-floor rear bedroom and was pronounced dead at Temple University Hospital.

The Inquirer printed what the police reported. I'm printing what the family knows. My grandfather did not walk twenty blocks. He walked to the corner, 20th and Willard Streets, steps from their front door, to put Donnetta on her school bus. He was gone minutes. The newspaper got that detail wrong. Fifty years later, as his granddaughter, I'm correcting the record.

What it cannot tell you, what no newspaper ever could, is what happened to our family in the aftermath of Troy's death. My parents, Ernest and Donna Willis, had been married since 1966. They were young. They were trying. They had built something on that block in North Philadelphia, a life with five children and a house and a future. And then October 23, 1975 took their firstborn son, and something between them broke that could never quite be repaired.

They separated. They never divorced, I don't know if that was faith, or stubbornness, or love in the only form it could still survive, but they struggled to live as husband and wife after Troy died in 1975. My mother raised us. My father remained in our lives, but the home as it had been was gone.

I was eight years old when I learned that the people you love can be here and then not here. That a morning can start ordinary and end with a casket. That grief doesn't destroy families all at once, sometimes it just quietly disassembles them, piece by piece, until one day you look around and realize everyone is still present but nothing is the same.

I filed all of that away. Eight-year-old Kim, standing on W. Willard Street in October 1975, watching the firemen work. Watching her mother's hands. Watching her grandfather's face.

I didn't know it then, but I was already learning the first lesson that would shape every career I would ever have.

> ***Some things cannot be navigated around. They can only be navigated through.***

THE OLDEST CHILD

I need to tell you something about being the oldest.

My full name is Kim Antionetta Willis. Born May 4, 1967, in Philadelphia, Pennsylvania, to Ernest Preston Willis and Donna Elizabeth Willis, née Thompson. First child. First experiment. The one the parents practiced on before they figured out what they were doing.

After Troy came Keary, then Gloria, then Tina. Four children who grew up in the shadow of a brother taken too soon. And above them all, the oldest, me, absorbing everything, watching everything, holding the family together in the quiet ways oldest children do without ever being asked or thanked.

My mother Donna was what I would call a force of nature wrapped in a peaceful smile. She died in 1998 of diabetic complications and her obituary recalls her as a warm, kind, and loving woman with a special sense of humor and a tremendous flair for life. That is absolutely true. But what the obituary couldn't capture was the steel underneath the warmth. The woman who attempted to scale a burning building. The woman who went on to raise four children after her marriage fell apart. The woman who, years later, would quit her job without hesitation to become a full-time grandmother to my son because she had decided his future mattered more than her paycheck.

That is the woman who raised me.

I am not bitter about my childhood. I want to say that clearly. I know what bitterness looks like, I've watched it eat people alive from the inside, and I made a decision somewhere along the way that I was not going to let loss become my identity. The fire. The separation. The grief that lived in our house like a permanent houseguest. All of it shaped me, yes. But shaped is different from damaged.

Being the oldest child in a family navigating grief taught me systems thinking before I knew what to call it. It taught me that someone has to keep track of things. Someone has to notice when things are going sideways before they go all the way wrong. Someone has to hold the center so that the edges don't fly apart.

That was always me. And it turns out, that skill travels. It travels to post offices. It travels to naval ships. It travels to healthcare systems. And it travels, very well, as it turns out, to artificial intelligence.

But I'm getting ahead of myself.

THE GIRL WHO WANTED TO BE A FORENSIC PATHOLOGIST

I graduated from high school in June 1985.

I was eighteen years old, pregnant, and absolutely certain that I was still going to become a forensic pathologist.

I had always been the curious one. The one who wanted to know not just what happened but why and how. Science made sense to me the way North Philadelphia street logic made sense to me, there were rules, and if you understood the rules deeply enough, you could predict the outcomes. Biology. Chemistry. The human body as a system. I was drawn to all of it. And forensic pathology, specifically, called to me in that particular way that a career calls to certain people, not as a job, but as a vocation. A way of giving voice to the dead. A way of finding truth in what the living couldn't explain.

I enrolled at Temple University as a biology major. Then a chemistry major. Then a biochemistry major. I was following the curiosity wherever it led, which in retrospect was less aimless wandering and more the mark of a mind that was genuinely hungry.

My son Dominic was born September 19, 1985.

I was eighteen, I had turned eighteen on May 4th of that year, four and a half months before he arrived. First-time mother. Full-time student. And as of January 1986, a part-time employee of the United States Postal Service, hired as a Casual Clerk at five dollars an hour because my mother, Donna Willis, the woman with the peaceful smile and the iron spine, was not going to allow her daughter's pregnancy to derail her future.

"You are going to college," she told me. It was not a question.

And so I went.

OCTOBER 12, 1985

Before I tell you about the Post Office, and Temple University, and the machine that kept jamming, before I tell you about the phone call that changed everything, I need to tell you about my father.

Ernest Preston Willis was born April 3, 1947. He married my mother in 1966 when they were both nineteen years old. He was, by all accounts and by my own memory, a man who loved his children and had enormous dreams for them. When he found out I was pregnant at seventeen, he was devastated, not because he stopped loving me, but because he knew exactly what I was capable of, and he was terrified that a baby would close doors he had always believed were open for me.

We argued. A real argument, the kind that cracks something. The kind where things get said that can't be unsaid, and then silence fills the space where the words used to be. After that argument, my father and I did not speak.

Dominic was born on September 19, 1985.

My father did not come to the hospital. He did not come in those first weeks. But he was in contact with my mother, they were separated, but they were still the parents of the same children, and Donna Willis was never the kind of woman to let a grudge stand between a grandfather and his grandson. She told me that my father had been asking about the baby. That he was going to bring him items that were not gifted at the baby shower, that he did not attend, for his grandson. He had told her he was planning to come by on Saturday, October 12th, to bring the gifts and to meet Dominic for the first time.

To end the silence.

Dominic was twenty-three days old on October 12, 1985.

My father never made it.

Earlier that day, in Burlington County, New Jersey, at a bar called Josh and Molly's, a woman named Franklyn Auslander, his ex-girlfriend, shot and killed my father, Ernest Preston Willis. She had told people she would do it. She had said that if she couldn't have him, nobody would. She made good on that promise on October 12, 1985, and then spent the next thirty years in a New Jersey prison for it.

My father was thirty-eight years old. He was buried on October 19, 1985, my brother Keary's fifteenth birthday, one week after he died, one month after his first grandson was born, exactly ten years and eleven days after his first son died.

He never got to hold my Dominic. He never got to say what he might have said, as he delivered arms full of baby shower gifts and his heart full of whatever it takes for a proud, hurt father to finally cross the threshold and reunite with his daughter.

I have spent a long time with that image. The gifts that never arrived. The door that never opened. The conversation that would have happened and now never will. The grandfather-less son.

> ***What I know is this: silence is a debt. And debt, if you leave it long enough, collects interest you never planned to pay.***

I don't argue. I don't raise my voice. I don't let disagreements harden into walls. People who know me wonder sometimes why I am so relentlessly committed to keeping things peaceful, to never letting distance grow where it doesn't have to. Now you know.

I watched what unresolved silence cost my family twice, once slowly, after Troy died in 1975, and once again in a single moment inside a bar in New Jersey in 1985. I decided very early that I was not going to add to that ledger.

That decision has shaped every relationship I have ever had. Every team I have ever led. Every client I have ever served.

THE MACHINE THAT KEPT JAMMING

By September 1986 I had made the transition from Casual Clerk to full-time regular employee at the United States Postal Service.

The pay went from five dollars an hour to eight dollars and nineteen cents. I was assigned to the automation unit at the main Post Office at 30th and Market Street in Philadelphia, working the evening shift, 3:50 PM to 12:20 AM. While I was at work, Dominic was with his grandmother Donna, with his father Greg, and with my siblings. The firstborn of the next generation, surrounded by people who loved him completely. He was, as my mother would say, thoroughly spoiled around the clock and not a bit sorry about it.

The automation unit was factory work, in my opinion. You stood at a machine. The machine sorted mail. The machine jammed. You cleared the jam. The machine sorted again. Eight hours of that, five days a week, and then you went home and started over.

I eventually dropped out of Temple University. Organic Chemistry II had something to do with that, I will be honest with you, that class had my full attention and still nearly broke me, but the deeper truth was that I couldn't be a full-time mother, a full-time postal worker, and a full-time student all at once. Something had to give. I told myself it was temporary. I told myself I would go back. The forensic pathologist dream didn't disappear, it just went into a drawer I didn't have time to open.

Three years into the Post Office, on September 5, 1989, I was standing at my machine on the fourth floor of the 30th Street Post Office when it jammed again. One technical failure after another, the kind of shift where nothing cooperates and the clock moves backward and you start having conversations with yourself about your life choices.

But the machine was not the only thing that had been jamming.

By 1988 I had my own apartment. Greg and I had ended things in early 1988. Not dramatically. Not badly. Greg had moved to the Washington DC area to help a cousin with his business, and for a while we tried to make the distance work. But distance has a way of doing what fear has already started. I had been afraid to marry him, afraid in the way that a woman becomes afraid when the only marriage she watched up close was her parents', two people who loved each other and could not survive the grief of losing a child together. Greg deserved a woman who could say yes without hesitation. I was not yet that woman. The distance gave us both permission to let go.

Giradie moved in.

Giradie was my first love. The person I had given my heart to before Greg, before Dominic, before any of the life that had accumulated around me. We had always found our way back to each other and this time felt no different. He moved in and for a while things were good, the way things can be good when you are young and in love and choosing to believe the best about the person sharing your space.

Then one afternoon he showed up at the Post Office to pick me up from work.

That was not normal. I took public transportation. We both knew that. So I asked him why he was there and he told me he had left his job, but he had something else lined up and just needed a week or two off before he started. It sounded reasonable. It was reasonable enough that I accepted it and we drove home and I did not think much more about it.

He started the new job. Things seemed fine.

Then he showed up at the Post Office again.

Same story. Left the job. Something else lined up. Needed a little time.

This time I heard it differently. Not because the words were different but because I was paying attention now in a way I had not been the first time. Something about the rhythm of it, the ease with which the explanation came, made me quiet in a way I could not quite explain.

I found out what the something else was.

Giradie had become a drug dealer. Street pharmaceuticals, as I came to think of it in my head, because calling it what it was felt too large and too close. He had decided that fast money was better than honest money, that the shortcut was worth the cost. He was wrong and I knew it the moment I understood what was happening.

I want to be clear about something. I am the young woman who still believed it was possible to become a forensic pathologist. I am the daughter of a woman who quit her job to raise my son so I could keep moving forward. I am the product of a family that had lost too much to lose anything more to choices that did not have to be made. Street pharmaceuticals were not my world, were never going to be my world, and I was not going to let them become my world by proximity.

I did not confront him in a dramatic way. I just knew. And knowing was enough.

The machine that kept jamming. The man whose path was going somewhere I would not follow. Two things that did not work, sitting side by side in my life, making the same quiet argument: Kim. It is time to go.

When break time came, we all took break together, factory-style, a whole bunch of us at once. I walked to the corridor by the elevators. Two pay phones. A window. I stood at that payphone and made a decision.

I called the Air Force recruiter.

I told him I wanted to enlist. I wanted to take my son somewhere new. I was ready to go by the end of the month, and I meant it, because I knew myself well enough to know that if I didn't move quickly I would talk myself out of it and have a whole new plan for the rest of my life.

The Air Force recruiter was kind. He was also honest. Single parent, he told me. No guarantee you could keep your son with you on deployment. He recommended I try the Navy, they tended to have more flexibility for situations like mine, he insisted.

I thanked him and hung up. Then I called the Navy.

By the time break was over, I had an appointment to take the Armed Services Vocational Aptitude Battery (ASVAB).

By September 28, 1989, only weeks after talking with the recruiter, I was standing at the Military Entrance Processing Station (MEPS) office at Broad and Cherry Street with my son Dominic, his father Greg, and my mother Donna Willis, the woman who had attempted to scale a burning building, who had outlasted grief, who had quit her job to raise my child so I could have a future, and I raised my right hand.

✦

I, Kim Willis, do solemnly swear that I will support and defend the Constitution of the United States against all enemies, foreign and domestic; that I will bear true faith and allegiance to the same; and that I will obey the orders of the President of the United States and the orders of the officers appointed over me, according to regulations and the Uniform Code of Military Justice. So help me God.

✦

Then I hugged my family. I hugged and held Dominic last, knowing that we would be reunited as soon as possible.

And I got on a plane to Orlando, Florida, my first plane ride in my entire life, headed to boot camp. I sat next to a young woman named Connie Kline. We were both headed off to a life of service in the United States Navy. Every time the plane hit turbulence on that flight, I grabbed her arm and apologized and grabbed it again.

I was twenty-two years old. I had a four-year-old son, a mother who believed in me with her whole chest, a father in a grave in Philadelphia, and a brother who had been gone for fourteen years. Another brother also in the

Navy. Two teenaged sisters still at home and eager to spoil Dominic in my absence.

I had no idea what I was doing.

I just knew I was done standing at a machine that kept jamming and I was preparing for a life of travel with my son.

THE LESSON

I could title this chapter a dozen different ways. The Making of a Navigator. The Education of Loss. What North Philadelphia Teaches You That College Cannot.

But here is what I actually learned in those first twenty-two years of my life, distilled down to its cleanest form:

Systems break. People break. Plans break. None of that is the end of the story unless you decide it is.

My brother Troy died in a burning house at age six. My parents' marriage didn't survive the grief. My father was killed before he could say what he needed to say. My dream of becoming a forensic pathologist went into a drawer like an old mismatched sock. Every single one of those things was real. Every one of them was loss.

And every single one of them taught me something that no classroom ever could about how to do KIM (Keep It Moving) when the machine jams. About how to stay present when the fire is real. About how the work of being human is not the absence of tragedy, it is the decision, made fresh every morning, to keep showing up anyway.

That's not a lesson I read in a book.

That's a lesson I learned standing on the Garretts' sidewalk on W. Willard Street in North Philadelphia, watching the smoke rise from my grandparents' house.

> ***Everything I would ever build,***
> ***every system I would ever run,***
> ***every team I would ever lead,***
> ***every client I would ever serve,***
> ***was built on that foundation.***

Now you know where and what Kim Willis comes from.

Let's keep going.

The Quartermaster

Boot camp in Orlando, Florida is hot.

I say that as someone who grew up in Philadelphia, where summers are no joke, but Orlando in the fall of 1989 had a different kind of heat to it. Heavy. Persistent. The kind that sits on your shoulders from the moment you step outside and does not let go until long after the sun goes down. I was twenty-two years old, I had just barely celebrated my son's fourth birthday on September 19 and on September 28 was leaving him, only temporarily, with his grandmother and his father, I had just taken an oath on the steps of the MEPS office at Broad and Cherry Street, and now I was standing in that Florida heat wondering exactly what I had gotten myself into.

The answer, it turned out, was something I needed.

Boot camp has one core purpose and the military does not try to hide it from you. The goal is to break you down as an individual so that you can be built back up as something more useful: a member of a team. A unit. A system. They strip away everything that made you who you were before you arrived, the habits, the attitude, the civilian mindset, and they replace it with something shared. A common language. A common standard. A common sense of what it means to show up and do your part.

There were push-ups. Many push-ups. More push-ups than I had any business doing in that Florida heat. Some of them were the standard issue kind that came with the program. Some of them were mine specifically, earned by what my fellow recruits and my superiors generously referred to as cockiness. I will not argue with the characterization. I was confident. I was capable. I knew it and apparently it showed, which is a thing that gets rewarded sometimes and punished with push-ups other times. In boot camp it was mostly push-ups.

What I will say in my own defense is that the confidence had a basis. I was selected as the Seaman Recruit Leading Petty Officer for my company. That is the recruit who steps up to lead the others, who is responsible for the unit's cohesion and performance, who answers for the group when things go right and when things go sideways. They do not give that role to someone who cannot handle it. They gave it to me.

There were drills and inspections and early mornings and nights where I cried into my pillow missing Dominic so much it felt physical, like something was actually missing from my chest. And then there was the day Aunt Joyce's icebox pound cake arrived at mail call.

She had packed it in a tin, wrapped beautifully the way only someone who loves you wraps something, and when my name was called and I opened that tin, the smell alone was enough to transport me straight back to Philadelphia. Aunt Joyce's icebox pound cake is not a store-bought situation. It is the real thing. The kind of thing you think about when you are standing in Florida heat doing push-ups far from everyone you love.

My Commander looked at the tin. Then he looked at me. Then he asked, very calmly, if I had enough for everybody.

I was still not quite getting it. I said no, my aunt only made this for me.

He explained, also very calmly, that if there was not enough for everybody then there was not enough for me.

I looked at my aunt's cake. I looked at my company. I understood.

There were no knives. There were no forks. There were no plates. There was just the tin and a company full of recruits who had not had anything homemade since they left home. We dug in. Everybody. With their hands. Into Aunt Joyce's icebox pound cake that she had made specifically for me and wrapped beautifully in a tin and sent all the way to Orlando, Florida.

I did not love sharing it. I will be honest about that. But I loved having it. And my shipmates loved it too, which I suppose is the whole point of the lesson. In the military nothing belongs to just you. The cake, the sacrifice, the mission, the grief, the victory. It all belongs to everybody. That is the system. Boot camp was just making sure I understood it before I got anywhere near a boat.

> ***They broke us down to build us up as a team. I had been doing that my whole life. I just finally had a name for it.***

I graduated boot camp and got my orders. San Diego, California. And I left one rank higher than I arrived.

I came in as an E1, Seaman Recruit. I walked out as an E2, Seaman, bumped up for outstanding performance as a recruit. The cockiness and the push-ups and the leading petty officer role had all added up to something the Navy decided was worth recognizing.

I had asked for overseas postings. London was on my dream list. All three of my preferred assignments were abroad. The Navy sent me to the exact opposite coast of the country instead, which at the time felt like a consolation prize and turned out to be one of the better things that ever happened to me, or so I thought.

My assignment was NOSC, the Naval Ocean Systems Center, in Point Loma, California. Just outside San Diego, sitting right at the edge of the Pacific, a place so different from North Philadelphia that I sometimes had to stop and remind myself that I was still in the same country.

I was not assigned to a ship. That surprises people when I tell them. When most people picture Navy life they picture a destroyer or an aircraft carrier, something large and gray cutting through the open ocean. What I was assigned to were boats. Specifically TWRs, Torpedo Weapons Retrievers. Small, functional, working vessels whose entire purpose was exactly what the name describes: we retrieved torpedoes after they had been fired during training exercises. NOSC had two TWRs, each with a crew of roughly the same size, and we would rotate and sub for each other when someone was on leave. We were one command, one family, spread across two boats.

My Petty Officer First Class was Arturo Camacho. He was in charge of our boat, the one running things, the one making sure the mission got done and the crew stayed straight. His second in command was Will, our Petty Officer Second Class. Between the two of them the boat was well run and I felt that from early on. Camacho and I are still Facebook friends to this day. That tells you something about the bonds this life builds.

Most of us lived together in the same barracks on base, with the exception of those who had families living in the area. That shared living was not incidental. It was part of what made us what we were. You cannot spend that much time that close to people, working the same rotation, eating in the same galley, sleeping down the hall from each other, and remain strangers. Boot camp breaks you down and builds you back up into a family. NOSC is where I understood what that actually meant in daily life.

Our rotation was simple and I came to love it. Two weeks out to sea, back every weekend. Then two weeks in port, working Monday through Thursday only, with a three-day weekend every week to balance out the time we spent underway without days off. It was structured. It was predictable. After a childhood and early adulthood built on anything but predictability, I found that rhythm deeply satisfying.

When I say out to sea, I mean a specific stretch of the Pacific Ocean between Point Loma and San Clemente Island. We called it the range. That is where the training exercises happened. That is where the torpedoes were fired and where we went to retrieve them.

Here is what nobody tells you about military service until you are already in it: some of it is genuinely, unexpectedly beautiful.

The TWR would take us out to the range and when the work called for it, we would deploy the zodiac. That is what we called it, the zodiac. One of those bright orange inflatable boats with the rigid hull and the raised sides, the kind you see in documentaries about rescues and expeditions. We would load into it and go out to retrieve the torpedoes after the exercises were done.

I want you to picture this: you are in a small orange boat on the Pacific Ocean. There is no land visible in any direction. Not a shoreline, not a rock, not a structure of any kind. Just water as far as you can see in every direction, and sky above it, and the boat under you, and the people next to you. The noise of the engine and the slap of the water against the hull and nothing else.

> ***I had left Philadelphia to see the world. Out on that zodiac, with no land anywhere in sight, I understood for the first time what that actually meant.***

My shipmate Baptista was usually out there with me. We rode that zodiac together more times than I can count and every single time it felt like freedom. Baptista was one of those people the military sends you, the ones you would never have met any other way, the ones who end up mattering more than you expected. He was my shipmate. He was my dude. The real ones are hard to find and he was one of them.

CHULA VISTA

In the early weeks at Point Loma I was staying on base in the barracks. It was fine. It was a kind of independence I had not had before, a different kind from what I had imagined but real nonetheless. I was figuring out what my life looked like without the familiar backdrop of North Philadelphia, and I was finding that I liked the answer.

Eventually Dominic came to California to be with me.

That sentence does not do justice to what that felt like. My son, four years old, flying across the country to start a new life with his mother in a place neither of us had ever been. I moved off base. My shipmate Travia Leatherwood and I got an apartment together in Chula Vista, a city just south of San Diego, close to the Mexican border, cleaner and quieter than anything I had known growing up. Her son had not yet come to live with her but mine was with me and the apartment was bright and the neighborhood was beautiful and for a stretch of time that

I still think about with warmth, everything felt like exactly what I had hoped it would be.

Chula Vista sits about fifteen minutes from the Mexican border, and back then, before restrictions tightened, military personnel could cross freely when there was no border restriction in place. So we did. Dominic and I went to Mexico together. We explored. We ate. We saw things. My sister Gloria came to visit once and the three of us went across together, a North Philadelphia girl and her boy and her sister, wandering through a foreign country on a Tuesday afternoon because we could.

I was carving out a life. A real one. Mine. And I was loving it.

TERRY

I need to stop here and tell you about Terry Wilkinson.

Terry was at our command. He was young, probably fresh out of high school, dark complexioned, wore his hair in a cut that went off to the side, the kind of style my son would wear years later. He was one of those people who just made things lighter by being in the room. Always around. Always part of whatever was happening. In a command as tight as ours, everybody knew everybody, and everybody knew Terry.

Terry Wilkinson had a habit with his Boondockers. Boondockers are the sturdy lace-up boots standard to Navy service, the ones you are supposed to lace up properly every time you put them on. Terry wore his like slippers. He would slip his feet in, slip his feet out, never tie them. It was his thing. Something small and personal and completely his own, the kind of quirk that becomes part of how people think of you.

One evening Terry was preparing for his watch on the boat. That is a routine part of Navy life: you stand your watch, you keep eyes on things, you do your part to make sure everything is secure through the night. Terry walked down the pier to board the boat for his watch.

With his Boondockers untied.

He fell over the side of the pier.

He drowned.

I am going to let that sit there for a moment because that is how it felt when it happened. No warning. No drama leading up to it. One moment Terry Wilkinson was walking down a pier the same way he had walked down piers a hundred times before, and then he was gone.

His best friend at the command, Redmond, took it the hardest. They did everything together, the two of them, the way certain friendships form in the military where you just become inseparable because you are going through the same thing in the same place at the same time. Losing Terry was losing half of something.

We all took it hard. That is what happens when a command becomes a family. The loss belongs to everyone.

> ***Boot camp teaches you that all you have is each other. Terry Wilkinson is why that lesson matters.***

I still think about him. The Gumby cut. The untied Boondockers. The way he was always just there, always part of the group, until he wasn't.

CHRISTMAS EVE, 1990

Now. Let me tell you about Christmas Eve 1990.

In the hood, stories like this one always start the same way: what had happened was.

What had happened was, it started that morning with work on the boat. We were removing and replacing the nonskid surface on the deck, the rough textured coating that keeps sailors from slipping on wet surfaces. The tool for this job is a pneumatic sander. You put it against the surface and you grind.

I was working my section when the sander went through my right knee.

I did not feel it. That is the part that stays with me. I looked down and saw blood, a significant amount of blood coming from my knee, and something happened in my body that my brain had not caught up to yet. I was going into shock.

Petty Officer Second Class Will was on watch. His job was keeping eyes on the crew and he saw what had happened before I fully processed it myself.

Baptista got there first.

What happened next I have told many times and it gets funnier every time, even though in the moment I was bleeding and confused and not laughing at all. Baptista came running over, grabbed my jeans at the knee and ripped them clean off from the knee down. Just tore them straight off. Then he started grabbing at my chest.

I want to be clear: I was in shock, bleeding from a serious knee wound, and suddenly also very busy fighting off my shipmate.

Will and the others were working on my knee, applying pressure, doing what needed to be done. Baptista, meanwhile, was determined and I was equally determined in the opposite direction. I was fighting him off with everything I had while simultaneously being treated for a knee injury, which in retrospect is a very Kim Willis way to handle a medical emergency.

When things settled enough for me to demand an explanation, Baptista told me the truth. He had learned that sudden unexpected contact was a technique for keeping a person in shock present and focused, pulling their attention away from the injury and the panic response. He was not trying to take advantage of a situation. He was, in his way, trying to keep me from going under.

I considered that. I looked at the evidence. And I concluded that Baptista is not a man who would do something like that with bad intentions. He was my shipmate. He did what he knew to do when it counted. Context matters. Intent matters. He achieved exactly what he set out to do: I stayed present, I got treated, I survived my own Christmas Eve pneumatic sander incident. I cannot be too upset about the method. We did share a laugh later, where he said to me that he had never had an opportunity to rip a woman out of her jeans until that day. If you know you know. Baptista was funny as heck.

The cut required four stitches underneath and eight stitches over the top. Twelve stitches total. On Christmas Eve. With Tylenol with codeine sent home with me for the pain.

Now. Here is where what had happened was gets interesting.

That evening, stitched up and officially off duty for the holiday, Baptista and Deanna Kaufman and a few other shipmates decided we were going to the movies in San Diego. The theater was running all the Godfather films back to back, all day, what today we would call a binge and what then we just called a very good reason to sit in a dark theater for several hours.

Now everybody, and I mean everybody, decided that we should not go to this Godfather marathon empty handed. So before we got to the theater, we made a stop. Vodka. Rum. Southern Comfort. Orange juice. Grapefruit juice. Cola. Cups. All of it smuggled into the movie theater in bags like we were bringing in a full bar service, which we were. The whole crew participated. That is what that kind of family does.

Throughout the Godfather marathon, we were serving each other mixed drinks in the dark like it was the most natural thing in the world.

My drink, my military drink, the one I had claimed as mine during my time in San Diego, was Southern Comfort and grapefruit juice. I will be honest with you: it is not a good drink. It is a nasty combination. But it was mine and I drank it.

I should mention, and this is important: I do not drink much. My father was an alcoholic and that shaped how I relate to alcohol from a young age. I have always had a two drink limit, sometimes one if it is strong, and in recent years I have barely touched it at all. On this particular Christmas Eve, I had my drinks during the Godfather marathon and called it a night.

What I did not account for was the Tylenol with codeine that was still very much active in my system from the knee surgery that morning.

We left the theater and went back to base. I went to my room. My roommate Stacey was away for the holiday, she was at a different command and had gone home, so I was alone. I laid down thinking I was going to sleep.

What had happened was, the Southern Comfort and the codeine introduced themselves to each other properly.

I could hear Kaufman banging on my door. In the military we call each other by last names and most people called me Willie instead of Willis. My friends called me Willie. So what I heard, from somewhere very far away, was Kaufman outside my door.

Hey Willie. Hey Willie.

I heard her. I tried to get up. I could not move. It felt like I was pinned to the bed, like gravity had doubled and my body was no longer accepting instructions. I was gargling on my own saliva, making sounds that were not words, completely unable to respond to the person on the other side of my door.

Kaufman was a Shorty. Petite. But she was rambunctious and rough around the edges in the best possible way and she was my homie. She did not wait for permission. She busted through that door.

She found me flat on my back, gargling, unable to move. She sat me upright. Saliva went everywhere. She started patting me on the back hard, the way you do when someone is choking, until I was breathing right and present and back in my own body.

Saved by my shipmates. Twice. Same day.

> ***I nearly died on Christmas Eve 1990. First from a pneumatic sander and then from Southern Comfort and codeine. Kaufman and Baptista between them kept me alive through both. That is what it means to have your people.***

I still have the scar on my right knee today. Every single day it is there. And every Christmas Eve I think about that theater, those Godfathers, that terrible drink, and the

Shorty who busted my door down and sat me up and saved my life.

THE FIRST HEADACHE

I want to be clear about something before I close this chapter.

The Navy was good to me. Not perfect. Not without its complications and its losses. But the core of it, the work and the water and the people and the life I was building in California with my son, that was good. That was real. That was what I came for.

I had chosen this. Standing at that payphone on the fourth floor of the 30th Street Post Office on a Saturday in September, I had chosen this over the machine that kept jamming. And the choice was right. I want that on the record.

What happened next was not the Navy's fault and it was not mine. It was just the body doing what bodies sometimes do: surprising you. Reminding you that no matter how carefully you plan, some variables are not yours to control.

The headaches started quietly, the way most things that are going to change your life start quietly. Not dramatic. Not sudden. Just a persistent pressure behind my eyes that was new and unfamiliar and would not go away.

I had never had headaches before in my life.

The neurologist visits started. Every four to six weeks, routine appointments, new medications each time, no relief in sight. The headaches kept coming. The medications kept changing. Something that had started as a manageable inconvenience was becoming a constant presence in my life.

I did not know yet what they meant. I did not know yet how much they were going to cost me. I did not know yet that the adventure I had worked so hard to build was about to become something more complicated.

I just knew my head hurt.

And I knew that something had shifted.

> ***The ocean was still out there. The zodiac was still waiting. But something in the picture had changed, and I could feel it even before I had words for what it was.***

The Headaches

I need you to understand something about me before I tell you what happened next.

I am a control freak. I say that without apology and without embarrassment because it is simply true. I am completely in control of myself. I lead from that place. I have built my entire life, every career, every relationship, every room I have ever walked into, on the foundation of knowing exactly who I am and exactly what I am doing. That self-possession is not arrogance. It is the thing that kept me standing when everything around me was falling.

So when I tell you that the migraines took that away from me, I need you to understand the full weight of what I am saying.

The headaches had started quietly at the end of Chapter 2. By the time we reach this chapter they were no longer quiet. They were constant. Relentless. A persistent pressure behind my eyes that no medication seemed to touch for long, that no amount of rest resolved, that became the unwanted background noise of every single day.

What followed was a rotating battery of medications that I can only describe as a pharmaceutical experiment conducted on my body one prescription at a time. Amitriptyline. Imitrex. Beta blockers. Others whose names I no longer remember because there were so many of them, each one presented as the answer, each one falling short. Every four to six weeks I was back in the neurologist's office. Every visit brought something new to try. Every new thing brought its own side effects, its own adjustments, its own version of not quite right.

I was not the only one at my command experiencing this.

I want to say that clearly because it matters. I was not an isolated case. Others around me were dealing with the same thing. Whether that means something or is simply coincidence, I cannot prove. I have no evidence. I have no answers. What I have is a pattern and a timeline: I never had a single headache in my life before I entered the United States Navy. My mother confirmed that. And now, decades later, I still have them. My daughter Victoria, who was conceived during this period, has them too. A medical professional would need to draw whatever conclusions they draw. I am simply telling you what I know.

> ***I went in healthy. I came out with headaches that never left. I am not***

> ***making an accusation. I am bearing witness to my own life.***

We were out on the range. One of those weeks between Point Loma and San Clemente Island, the routine that had become as familiar to me as breathing. The work, the water, the crew, the zodiac. I was on one of the medications, I cannot tell you which one specifically because by this point they had blurred together into a constant rotation of try this, try that, and I had largely stopped tracking the names.

And then something happened that I still find difficult to fully explain.

I was sitting in the galley on the boat. My crew was around me. These were my people, the men and women I had stood watch with and ridden zodiacs with and shared a barracks with and counted on the way you can only count on people when you have been broken down and built back up alongside them. I knew them. They knew me.

And I started cursing them out.

Not a word here and a sharp tone there. All of them. Everything I had apparently been keeping somewhere inside me came out in a way that was not mine, in a voice I did not recognize as my own, directed at people who had done nothing to deserve it. I told them exactly how I felt about them, or so it may seem. I was not gentle. I was not measured. I was not Kim Willis.

That last part is the part that still gets me.

I am not a person who curses people out. I am not a person who loses control of my words. I am not a person who does not know, at every moment, exactly what is coming out of her mouth and why. I have lived by that discipline since I was eight years old standing on the Garretts' sidewalk watching things fall apart around me and deciding I was not going to add to the chaos. I have raised my voice at no one. I have argued with no one. I carry my father's story in my body as a permanent reminder of what silence costs and what rage costs and I have chosen, every day of my adult life, to be neither.

What happened in that galley was not me. It was a medication doing something to my brain that I did not consent to and could not control.

And then, as suddenly as it started, it stopped.

And I broke down crying.

The crying was mine. The devastation at what had just come out of me, the confusion, the grief of not knowing what was happening inside my own head, that was all me. I was emotional and lost and frightened in a way I had not been since I was a child. A woman who had crossed the country alone, raised a son, enlisted in the United States Navy, earned a rank bump at boot camp, ridden a zodiac into open ocean with no land in sight, was sitting in a galley on a boat in the Pacific Ocean completely unable to account for what she had just done.

> ***A control freak with no control left. That is what those medications did to me. And I knew, sitting there, that something had to change.***

THE ROOF OF BALBOA NAVAL MEDICAL CENTER

They airlifted me from San Clemente Island to Balboa Naval Medical Center in San Diego.

A United States Navy helicopter. My first helicopter ride ever, and as it turned out, my only one.

I remember being at the sick bay on the island and being told what was going to happen. I remember the word airlifted and the way it registered as something that happened to other people, to people in serious situations, not to me. Not for headaches. Not for a medication reaction. And yet there I was.

I remember the flight in the way you remember things when you are not fully present for them, in fragments and impressions rather than a clean continuous memory. The noise of the rotors. The particular quality of light. The strange remove of looking at the ocean from above, that same Pacific I had been riding across in a zodiac, now spread out underneath me like a map of something I could not quite read.

I remember landing on the roof of Balboa Naval Medical Center. I remember a wheelchair. I remember being wheeled somewhere, through corridors, past people who moved with purpose while I moved with none. I was emotional. I was still not entirely in my own body. A woman who prided herself on knowing exactly where she stood in every room she entered had no idea where she was or what came next.

I believe I was taken directly to Captain Catron. He was my treating physician, my neurologist, the one who had been managing the medication rotation since this whole thing began. If anyone was going to make sense of what had happened on that boat, it was going to be him.

I want to tell you that I arrived at his office composed and articulate. I want to tell you that I explained the situation clearly and professionally and that we had a measured clinical discussion about next steps.

That is absolutely not what happened.

I cussed him out too, yes him too.

I know. I know. Insubordination does not begin to cover it. Captain Catron was a United States Navy officer, a ranking officer, and my treating physician, and I sat across from him and I gave him a piece of my mind that I did not have the rank or the standing to give. I told him what I thought about the medications that were not working. I told him what I thought about feeling like a different person inside my own skin. I told him I was tired, that I was done, that I just wanted to go home.

Captain Catron listened.

And when I was done he said to me, simply and without any of the defensiveness my outburst probably warranted:

> ***You will. And I will help you.***

I have thought about those seven words many times in the years since. The patience they required. The discernment to hear the truth underneath the anger, to understand that a woman who cursed out her neurologist was not a discipline problem but a person in genuine distress who needed someone to hear her.

Captain Catron submitted a request for a medical discharge on my behalf.

Before I get to the discharge, I need to tell you about the Persian Gulf.

When the war erupted, the military was looking for volunteers. That distinction mattered to me. Being asked to go as a volunteer felt different from being arbitrarily selected and sent. I wanted to go. I had entered the Navy to serve, to travel, to be part of something larger than a machine on the fourth floor of the 30th Street Post Office. The Persian Gulf was exactly the kind of assignment I had signed up for.

I put my name in. I went through the process, completed the request, sat across from someone who seemed genuinely glad to have volunteers raising their hands rather than having to point at people. The energy in those conversations was good. I believed I was going.

I was denied.

The reason was the migraines. I could not be stationed overseas. I had to remain within the continental United States at all times, near a medical facility, because of the ongoing neurological situation. That was the ruling and there was no appeal that was going to change a medical determination.

I sat with that for a long time.

I had come into the Navy with a dream list. London. Overseas. Somewhere other than where I had always been. The Navy had sent me to San Diego instead of London, which turned out to be my consolation prize. Now the Navy was telling me I could not go anywhere at all, that the headaches that had arrived uninvited in my body had effectively grounded me for the duration of my service.

That was the moment the adventure became a job.

I want to be precise about what I mean by that. The work did not change. My crew did not change. The zodiac and the range and Camacho and Baptista and everything I had built in California, none of that changed. What changed was the horizon. The sense of possibility that had carried me from that payphone on the fourth floor of the 30th Street Post Office all the way to Point Loma, California. That horizon closed.

And when the horizon closes, what you have left is a job.

I had left a job in Philadelphia. I was not going to stay in the military just to have another one.

> ***"It's not just a job. It's an adventure." I went into the Navy for the adventure. The adventure had just become a job. And if it was just a job, I might as well go home.***

I took leave and flew home to Philadelphia.

I want to be honest with you about what I went home to do, because this book is built on honesty and I am not going to soften this particular truth.

I went home intending to get pregnant.

I had thought about it with the kind of clarity that comes when you have already made a decision and are simply working out the logistics. Getting pregnant as a single parent would accelerate my path home. It was a plan, deliberate and considered, made by a woman who had run out of other options that felt like her own.

The man I went home to was Giradie. My first love. The person whose life choices had been part of what sent me into the military in the first place. We had always found our way back to each other, and he was willing, more than willing, to bring a life into the world with me. That part was never in question.

What he was not willing or able to do was be the father that child deserved. Victoria has no relationship with him today. Neither do I. And if she ever reads these pages and wonders why I am telling this part of the story, I want her to know: I have never been ashamed of how she came into this world. I made a choice. She is the best thing that came from it.

I went back to California after my leave. I requested a pregnancy test.

It was positive.

I was going to have a daughter.

I did not know that yet, of course. But Victoria was already there, already becoming, already carrying whatever would come with her into this world. I just knew I was pregnant, that I was going home, and that God, as He had done in my life more times than I can count, had looked out for me even when I was not entirely looking out for myself.

YOU WILL

The discharge process took time, the way military processes take time, with paperwork and reviews and the particular patience required when an institution built for permanence begins the process of releasing someone.

Captain Catron was as good as his word.

He had heard me. Not just the anger and the frustration, but the truth underneath it: that the medications were not working, that I was not myself, that the adventure had become something I no longer recognized as my own life. He had looked at the whole picture and concluded that the right thing to do was help me go home with my dignity intact.

I was discharged from the United States Navy in July 1991 with an honorable discharge on medical grounds. My disability rating was ten percent.

Ten percent.

I want to sit with that number for a moment because it has a longer story attached to it. I came in ready to give my life and my career to this institution. I left with a medical condition that has never resolved, medications that changed who I was in my own body, a daughter conceived partly because service overseas was no longer an option, and a disability rating of ten percent. Other women from my command left with military retirement. I did not receive what I felt I deserved and the reasons given were that things had not been properly submitted.

That fight, the long fight for proper recognition, continued for years after I left California. It was not resolved quickly. It was not resolved easily. And it should not have had to be fought at all by a woman who raised her right hand and meant every word of the oath she took. But it was fought. And it was eventually won.

But that is a chapter for another book.

For this one, I want to end here: Captain Catron did right by me when he did not have to. He heard a woman who was out of options and out of patience and probably out of line by any military standard, and he chose to help her anyway. I am grateful for that. I carry that gratitude the same way I carry the scar on my right knee, every single day, without having to remind myself it is there.

> ***Sometimes the person who helps you out is the one you least expected to, after you have already given them every reason not to.***

THE LESSON

I did not get everything I came for.

I did not get London. I did not get the Persian Gulf. I did not get the military career I had imagined standing at that payphone in September 1989. I got San Diego and a zodiac and Camacho and Baptista and Kaufman and Wilkinson and Leatherwood and many others and an icebox pound cake eaten with bare hands in a Florida barracks and twelve stitches on Christmas Eve and a helicopter ride over the Pacific and a daughter and a neurologist who said "you will and I will help you".

That is not nothing. That is, in fact, a great deal.

Here is what the Navy taught me that no classroom, no Post Office, no amount of North Philadelphia street sense could have taught me on its own: there are things you cannot control and systems bigger than you that will make decisions about your life that you did not ask for and cannot appeal. You can volunteer for the Persian Gulf and be told no. You can take medication that changes who you are. You can do everything right and still get a ten percent rating when you deserved more.

What you do with that, how you carry it, whether you let it make you bitter or whether you let it make you wise, that is the only variable that belongs to you.

I chose wise. I am still choosing it.

KIM. Keep It Moving.

> ***The Navy gave me more than it took. And what it took, it took from a woman strong enough to survive the taking.***

The Long Way Home

Before I could drive home I had to send my son ahead.

Dominic flew back to Greg before my discharge was complete. I want to be clear that this was not a tearful, uncertain goodbye. By the time we reached the summer of 1991 Dominic was practically a veteran traveler in his own right. He had flown across the country. He had flown out to California with my sister Gloria. He had made the short forty-five minute hop between PHL and BWI so many times, shuttling between me and Greg when Greg was living in the Washington DC area, that the airport staff knew how to handle him and he knew how to handle the airport.

That was one of the agreements Greg and I had worked out between us after things ended. Equal time. And rather than making Dominic bear the three-hour drive between Philadelphia and DC every time, we would put him on a plane by himself under the airport's supervision. I would walk him to the gate, settle him in, and leave. Greg would be waiting when he landed. Then it would reverse. A forty-five minute flight for a four-year-old flying solo sounds dramatic until you understand that Dominic had been navigating the world with a kind of easy confidence since before he could fully explain it. He came by that naturally.

So when it was time for him to fly back east ahead of my discharge, he went the way he always went: without drama, without fear, as though the world had been arranged for his convenience and he saw no reason to question it.

I, on the other hand, had a U-Haul to pack.

THE TRIPTIK

I need to tell you something about the summer of 1991 that younger readers may not fully appreciate.

There was no GPS.

There was no WAZE or Google Maps. There was no phone in your pocket that could recalculate your route in real time or tell you where the nearest gas station was or warn you that you were about to run low in the middle of the Arizona desert. There was paper. There were road signs. And if you were smart and organized and a member, there was AAA TripTik.

The American Automobile Association, AAA, offered a service where you could come in, tell them your starting point and your destination, and they would map out your entire route by hand, highlighting the roads you should take across every state you would pass through. You had to request it ahead of time and wait a few days for it to be ready. Then you would go back and pick it up: a stack of maps, each one covering a section of your journey, each one with your specific route highlighted in bright color so you could follow it through territory you had never seen.

I went to AAA. I requested my TripTik. I waited. I picked it up.

San Diego, California to Philadelphia, Pennsylvania. Approximately 2,700 miles. Alone, in a U-Haul truck, with a stack of paper maps and the absolute determination of a woman who had navigated a Navy boat through open ocean and was not about to be defeated by an interstate highway.

> ***A Quartermaster navigates by the tools available. In 1991, the tools were paper, signs, and the willingness to trust the route even when you could not see what was coming next.***

U N D E R W A Y

I left San Diego in early July 1991 with my belongings loaded into the back of a U-Haul and my TripTik on the seat beside me.

I was not in a hurry. That is important to understand about this drive. I did not push hard to get home. I had been calling the family along the way so they could track my progress, and I had given them a general sense of when to expect me, but I was not racing. I had spent the better part of two years operating on a military schedule, someone else's clock, someone else's rotation. This drive was mine. The road was mine. The pace was mine.

When I was tired I pulled over and rested. When something caught my eye I stopped and looked. I saw things on that drive that I had only ever seen in books. Landscapes that did not look real until you were standing inside them. The particular silence of the Southwest desert at a certain hour of the morning. The way the light changes as you move through different terrain, the sky seeming to get bigger and then bigger again until you understand why people who grew up under it cannot quite explain to those who did not what the difference feels like.

I was a girl from North Philadelphia. Inner-city blocks had been my world for the first twenty-two years of my life. And now I was alone in a U-Haul somewhere between California and Arizona watching the country open up around me like something I had been promised and was only now collecting.

> ***I had gone into the Navy to see the world. The world had sent me home by the long way. I was not complaining.***

Somewhere in Arizona, my TripTik and the highway signs conspired to deliver me a very important piece of information: if I did not stop at the next available gas station, I was going to run out of gas in the desert.

The next available gas station was not what I would have called a gas station in any context I had previously known.

I had been following what I believe were train tracks for a stretch of road that felt like it led nowhere. The terrain was dusty and wide and the kind of beautiful that is also slightly threatening if you are a woman alone in a U-Haul who has not seen another vehicle in a while. And then, emerging from the landscape like something out of an old film, there it was.

An old pump. The kind you see in movies set in the 1940s, the kind that looks like it predates every gas station I had ever been to in Philadelphia. Connected to what appeared to be a local spot, a small place where the regulars came in for breakfast or lunch, with one of those old soda machines outside that still dispensed bottles the way they used to before everything became plastic and automated. A few older white residents sitting around with the particular ease of people who had been there a long time and were not expecting company.

And me. In a U-Haul. With a Philadelphia accent. Possibly the most out of place person that gas station had seen in some time.

I could not figure out the pump. I want to be clear that I had been pumping my own gas since I was eighteen years old. This was not a skill gap. This was a technology gap. The pump operated on a logic I had never encountered and I stood there long enough that a young boy, maybe ten or eleven years old, came out to help me.

His name was Randy.

Randy pumped my gas without making me feel foolish about it, which I appreciated. What I also noticed, and still think about, was the reaction from the older folks watching from nearby. As Randy worked, someone started up a singsong little chant.

Randy's got a girlfriend. Randy's got a girlfriend.

He was a child trying to help a stranger. They were adults making it into something else. I took note of that. I took note of the fact that I might have been one of very few Black people those particular individuals had ever seen up close, and that their idea of how to handle that moment was to embarrass a little boy who was just being kind.

Randy did not seem bothered. He finished the job, took the payment, and that was that.

I drove away thinking about him. About the particular grace of a child who has not yet learned to perform discomfort around people who look different from him. About the difference between the world Randy was growing up in and the world I wanted Dominic to know.

> ***Randy pumped my gas and did not make me feel like a stranger. That was enough. Sometimes enough is everything.***

85 IN A 60

New Mexico was beautiful.

I say that first because it is true and because what comes next might overshadow it if I do not establish the beauty up front. The drive through New Mexico, the particular quality of the light there, the way the land sits at elevation and the air feels different in your chest, was one of the more striking stretches of the whole trip. Santa Fe sits at over seven thousand feet above sea level and it shows. Everything looks slightly more vivid there. Colors are sharper. Shadows are longer.

I was appreciating all of this at approximately eighty-five miles per hour in a sixty mile per hour zone.

I was not doing this intentionally. Or rather I was not aware of doing it. The U-Haul and I had come to an understanding somewhere around Arizona and apparently that understanding included a cruising speed that New Mexico's highway patrol found objectionable.

I saw the officer's vehicle on the other side of the road as I passed. By the time he had processed what he was seeing, turned around, gotten off at an exit, turned around again, and come back down the highway to catch me, I had covered six additional miles. This is what he told me when he finally pulled me over. It took me six miles just to catch up to you and I did not know a U-Haul went that fast.

I had been trained. Before you show your driver's license, show your military ID. So when he asked for my license, registration, and paperwork, I produced my military ID first and then made a show of searching through the rest of my documents while he had a moment to register it. He registered it. He told me he respected the military.

He also gave me a ticket.

The ticket was also an envelope. Outside the envelope was everything you needed to handle it: instructions for paying, a place to write your check, and a checkbox if you wanted to contest it and appear in court. I considered that checkbox for approximately as long as it took me to understand that I had no intention of ever returning to Santa Fe, New Mexico to argue about a speeding ticket.

I wrote the check. I mailed it when I got home to Philadelphia. I do not remember the amount. I remember that it was my first and only speeding ticket, that the officer was decent about it, and that somewhere in New Mexico there is a copy of a citation showing the day Kim Willis drove a U-Haul like she was late for something important.

She was not late. She was just free.

ALMOST HOME

I stopped for the night somewhere in Pennsylvania, around Harrisburg, when I had been on the road for a couple of days. I had been calling home at intervals along the way so my family could track where I was, and by the time I settled in for that last night's rest they knew approximately when to expect me.

The drive through West Virginia had been something. The Appalachians after the flat wide Southwest were a different kind of beautiful, green and close and almost overwhelming after days of desert and sky. The country kept changing the whole way home and I kept watching it change, storing it away the way I had always stored things away since I was eight years old on the Garretts' sidewalk, building the internal archive that would eventually become the person writing these words.

The last stretch of Pennsylvania felt familiar in a way nothing had felt for months. The particular shade of green. The way the sky sat lower and closer. The highway signs counting down miles to Philadelphia with the matter-of-fact efficiency of a city that has never been particularly sentimental about its own existence.

I was twenty-four years old. I had a son who was a frequent flyer. I had a daughter growing quietly inside me, not yet showing, not yet named, already present. I had an honorable discharge, a ten percent disability rating, a scar on my right knee, and two years of a life that had taken me from North Philadelphia to Orlando to San Diego to San Clemente Island and back across the entire country in a U-Haul I had apparently been driving at criminal speeds.

I pulled onto W. Willard Street.

My grandfather was sitting on the porch.

I need you to understand what that image meant before I try to describe it. My entire childhood had been organized around that porch, that house, that man. Four doors away at 1933 W. Willard, Hebrew Thompson had been a fixed point in a world that kept moving and shifting and taking things away. His house was where Troy had been. His porch was where you could find him on a summer evening, the same way you could always find him, the same way certain people become so consistent in your life that their presence starts to feel like weather, like something you stop noticing because it has always simply been there.

He was sitting in his chair. On his head was my NOSC ball cap.

I have a photograph of this that I keep because some moments deserve to be kept in more than one form. My grandfather in that chair with my Navy cap on his head, and my grandmother Gloria sitting on the arm of the same chair, leaning into him the way people lean into each other when they have been doing it for so long it has become part of how they hold themselves upright. The two of them together, the way they had always been, waiting for me to come home.

My grandfather had been proud when I got the Post Office job. A good government job, he had said, with the particular satisfaction of a man who understood what stable employment meant in a world that had not always offered it freely. He had been proud when I went into the Navy, another kind of service, another kind of steadiness. He was a veteran himself. My brother Keary had gone into the Navy before me and we had even overlapped briefly in San Diego before he transitioned out. Service was not foreign to this family. It was something we did.

I do not remember exactly what my grandfather said when I pulled up. I remember the feeling of it, which was something like relief that had been held so long it had forgotten it was relief until it was finally released. I had been gone and now I was back. I was almost like I had never left, except that I had, and the me that was pulling up to that porch in a U-Haul was not the same me that had stood at a payphone on the fourth floor of the 30th Street Post Office two years before.

She was different. She was wider. She had seen open ocean from a zodiac and desert from a highway and the roof of a naval hospital from a helicopter. She had been broken down in boot camp and built back up as something more than she had been. She had lost shipmates and gained family and cussed out a United States Navy officer and been airlifted from an island and driven 2,700 miles alone with a stack of paper maps and the stubborn conviction that she knew where she was going even when she did not.

That woman pulled up to 1933 W. Willard Street and saw her grandfather sitting on the porch in her Navy cap and felt, for the first time in a long time, that she was exactly where she was supposed to be.

> ***Full circle does not mean you end up where you started. It means you return to the place you began as someone who has earned the right to be there.***

DECEMBER 16, 1991

Victoria was born on December 16, 1991.

She came into the world the same way Dominic had: by emergency C-section, after going into fetal distress when I did not dilate enough for a vaginal delivery. Both of my children arrived the same way, urgent and necessary and not particularly interested in following the expected route. I cannot say I was surprised. They came from me.

What I did not expect was the company.

My baby sister Tina and I had been pregnant at the same time. We had carried our babies through the same months, compared notes, occupied the same family conversations about due dates and names and what came next. And on December 16, 1991, a date that neither of us were due, we both went into labor.

Same day. Same hospital.

Tina's son Marc arrived after midnight. Victoria arrived at noon. Twelve hours apart, same building, the Willis women doing what the Willis women have always done: showing up together, refusing to let the important moments happen without each other.

I looked at my daughter and I thought about the road that had brought her here. The payphone on the fourth floor. The oath at MEPS. The zodiac on the range. The helicopter over the Pacific. The U-Haul through the desert. Randy pumping my gas. The ticket in Santa Fe. My grandfather on the porch in my Navy cap.

All of it had led to this: a girl born on the same day as her cousin, in the same hospital as her aunt, into a family that was already waiting.

Her name was Victoria.

She had already survived more than she knew.

THE LESSON

Chapter 4 is the chapter where Act One ends.

The Quartermaster years are done. The Navy is done. The uniform is hung up. The woman who left North Philadelphia in September 1989 with a four-year-old son, a TripTik she had not yet requested, and a life she was in the process of building, has come back to the block she started on.

She is not the same.

Here is what the drive home taught me, beyond the speeding ticket and the gas pump and the boy named Randy and the green of West Virginia after the desert:

The road is never wasted. Not one mile of it. Every stretch of empty highway, every unfamiliar landscape, every moment of navigating without a GPS and with nothing but paper maps and road signs and your own best judgment, that is all data. That is all experience. That is all yours.

I had gone into the military to travel. I had been grounded by migraines. I had driven myself home through seven states because the adventure owed me a ending I could choose for myself, and a 2,700 mile solo drive in a U-Haul was exactly the kind of ending that Kim Willis would choose.

You do not need someone's permission to take the long way home. Sometimes the long way is the only way that teaches you what you needed to learn.

> ***I left North Philadelphia to see the world. The world sent me home with migraine headaches, a daughter, a scar, a stack of paper maps, and a story worth telling.***

Act Two returns me to the Post Office.

Let's keep going.

The Mastery

I want to tell you something about how I found out I did not have to come home.

When I was preparing to leave the Navy in the summer of 1991 I contacted the Post Office and asked whether I could simply be reinstated at a facility in California. I had built a life in San Diego. My son and I were adjusting to California. It seemed a reasonable question. The answer I was given at the time was clear: no, I had to return to the Post Office I had left in Philadelphia. That was the rule. That was the process. So I packed up a U-Haul, drove 2,700 miles across the country, and reported to the main Post Office at 30th and Market Street in Philadelphia to be reinstated.

Then human resources told me the rule I had been given was wrong. I could have stayed in California. The military would not have paid my travel back to Philadelphia, but there had been no regulation requiring me to return to my original office. The information I had acted on was incorrect.

I sat with that for a moment.

And then I did what I have always done when something happens that I did not choose and cannot undo. I looked for what God might be showing me in it. I believe, with everything I have, that my life is not governed by other people's decisions or mistakes. I believe I am where I am supposed to be when I am supposed to be there. So I was back in Philadelphia. Back at the 30th Street Post Office. Back on the automation floor, now the third floor instead of the fourth, surrounded by machines that had multiplied and evolved in the two years I had been gone.

I was not going to stand at a machine again. Not permanently. I had come back to the Post Office but I had not come back to be who I was when I left it.

> ***I returned to the Post Office the same way I returned to everything: as someone who had earned more than what was waiting for me there, and intended to collect it.***

THE WINDOW CLERK

I did not stay on the automation floor for long. Within a year I found my way to a city station, which in the postal world means a neighborhood post office as opposed to the main processing facility. My first station was Overbrook, located in the Overbrook section of Philadelphia.

The difference was immediate and felt right. At the main Post Office you were a component in a factory. The mail moved through you on its way to somewhere else. At a city station you were the face of the Post Office to a specific community. Customers came in with their packages and their money orders and their questions and their frustrations, and you were the person who either helped them or did not. That human contact, that direct accountability to real people in a real neighborhood, suited me in a way the automation floor, factory atmosphere, never had.

My title was window clerk, a name that would later transition to Sales, Services and Distribution Associate as the Postal Service updated its language if not always its practices. Whatever you called it, the job was clear: serve the customers, know the products, handle the finances, and represent the institution with competence every single day.

I was good at it. I moved eventually to Spring Garden Station, another Philadelphia neighborhood office, and it was there that the next chapter of my postal career quietly began to take shape.

THE STEWARD

I became a union steward again, as I had been prior to leaving for the United States Navy, for a reason that had nothing to do with politics and everything to do with justice.

There were people around me, coworkers, colleagues, good postal workers who knew when something was wrong and who would complain about it to everyone they knew except the one person who could actually do something about it. I understood that impulse. Not everyone is equipped to stand in front of management and make an argument. Not everyone knows their rights well enough to defend them. Not everyone has the particular combination of confidence and preparation that makes those confrontations feel survivable.

I had all of that. I had always had all of that. So again I joined the American Postal Workers Union, known as the APWU, and became a steward, which meant I became the person who showed up for the people who could not show up for themselves.

I studied that contract the way I had once studied biochemistry at Temple University, with the genuine hunger of a person who understood that knowledge was power and that power, in the right hands, could protect people. I attended meetings. I went to conventions when the opportunity arose. I knew the APWU contract thoroughly enough that management took notice. There is a dynamic that develops in workplaces when someone knows the rules better than the people enforcing them, and

I came to understand it well: they would rather have you on their side than across from them.

Which is how I ended up becoming an acting supervisor.

It was not officially stated that way. Nobody called me into an office and said Kim, we want you in management because you are too dangerous as a steward. But we all understood the logic. Union stewards who know the contract inside and out make excellent members of management. They understand what the workers are entitled to, what the institution is required to provide, and where the lines are that nobody should cross. That knowledge does not disappear when you change sides of the table. It just becomes more useful in a different direction.

> ***The best managers I ever knew understood the contract. The worst ones hoped nobody else did.***

MR. COLEMAN

The person who gave me the opportunity to become an acting supervisor at Spring Garden Station was Eric Coleman.

Mr. Coleman was the kind of manager who taught you things without always announcing that he was teaching you. One of the most valuable lessons I carry from him has nothing to do with postal operations or contract language. It has to do with how you see people.

When I came to work for Mr. Coleman, I had what could generously be described as a substantial disciplinary file. The manager before him, a person whose name I have no interest in putting in these pages, had used my medical absence to compile every possible notice and write-up he could generate, building a record that was less an accurate portrait of my performance and more a monument to his own hostility. That file preceded me. People knew about it. And Mr. Coleman looked at it and set it aside.

He told me something I have never forgotten. He said he did not give weight to other people's experiences with someone when forming his own opinion. Just because the previous manager and I had not gotten along did not mean that he and I would not. He was going to find out for himself who Kim Willis was. He was not going to let someone else's conflict become his bias.

I have carried that into every leadership role I have held since. Two people can have a difficult relationship that tells you nothing about how either of those people will relate to a third. You do not inherit other people's judgments. You form your own. That is not just good management. That is good character.

Mr. Coleman saw something in me worth developing and he gave me the room to develop it. I have not forgotten that, and I have tried to be that kind of leader for others ever since.

DISNEY WORLD

Christmas 1993. Victoria and Marc had just turned two. The same babies born on the same day in the same hospital two years before were now toddlers with opinions and energy and the particular chaos that two-year-old twins would generate if they had been twins, which they were not, but which they might as well have been given how inseparable they were.

Tina and I decided we were taking the children to Disney World for Christmas. Dominic was eight. Marc and Victoria were two. Five of us in the car, me and my sister and our three children, headed to Florida for the kind of holiday that would give the babies something to remember even if they were probably too young to fully remember it.

We were rear ended in Lumberton, South Carolina. The vehicle was totaled. We did not make it to Disney World in that car.

We took a Greyhound bus.

Let that sit there for a moment. Rear ended, vehicle totaled, bumps and bruises and pain on every one of us, and we had only been seven hours away from Disney World when it happened. Seven hours left on an eighteen-hour drive from Philadelphia, and my car was gone. Tina and I looked at each other and looked at those three children and decided that we had come too far to turn around and go home. So we got on a Greyhound bus in Lumberton, North Carolina. What should have been seven more hours turned into an eighteen hour reset. Every small town between us and Orlando had a bus station, and we stopped at all of them. The ride felt endless. We were hurting. We were exhausted. And we kept going anyway.

I say walked. Tina and I struggled to walk. We were hurting. We were exhausted. We were the kind of sore that comes from absorbing a car crash with your body and then sitting on a bus for eighteen hours. But we put on our faces for the children and we did Disney World, because that is what you do when you believe that the things that happen to you are not the end of the story.

I have said throughout this book that when things occur that I did not choose, I look for what God is showing me in them. The Christmas 1993 accident was no different. We did not make it to Disney World in my car we drove down in. We made it in spite of everything that tried to stop us. Marc and Victoria had their first Disney World Christmas. Dominic, eight years old and probably slightly bewildered by the entire sequence of events, was there too. For Dominic, this was yet another trip to Disney World. And Tina and I, bruised and tired and absolutely not going home without having done what we came to do, stood in that park and watched those babies and called it a win.

I was injured badly enough that returning to work was not immediately possible. I went out on medical leave with legitimate restrictions that my doctor documented carefully. What I did not anticipate was the response from the manager I was working under at the time at Spring Garden Post Office, whose name I will not include because he has already taken enough from me and I will not give him space in my book too.

He did not accommodate my restrictions. He assigned me work that my body physically could not perform, work that a reasonable person with any concern for their employee's wellbeing would not have assigned to someone with documented medical limitations. I asked him once, directly, whether he would ask his mother, who had been through what I had been through, to do the same things he was asking of me.

He did not answer the question. My doctor answered it instead, by removing me from work entirely on the grounds that the Post Office was not cooperating with my recovery.

From that point forward, the manager compiled a file. Every absence, every notice, every piece of paper he could generate in my direction while I was out under medical care went into a growing record that he apparently believed would give him grounds to remove me from the Postal Service entirely.

He was wrong. But it took time to prove it.

During that time, I went back to Temple University. My doctor had me home. The Post Office had given me a reason to be angry. I chose to be productive instead. I sat back in those lecture halls and classrooms and worked on the degree I had put in a drawer years before, the forensic pathologist's dream that had never entirely stopped being a dream even when life had made it temporarily impossible.

The Post Office eventually determined there was no basis for removal. All benefits were restored. A year's salary came back to me as a lump sum. The unnamed manager had spent considerable energy trying to end my career and had accomplished nothing except giving me time to further my education.

Years later, I saw the same manager, after his Postal Service retirement at my local bank branch working as a teller. It was a sort of awkward moment, but I tried to dismiss it as quickly as I could.

> ***The Post Office tried to fire me and gave me a year's salary instead. That is not failure. That is the universe correcting its own math.***

THE MONEY ORDER

It happened again.

A customer purchased a money order. I imprinted the wrong amount, a clerical error, the kind of mistake that the Postal Service's own process made unnecessarily difficult to correct. I caught it immediately. I notified my T6, which is the person responsible for collecting and reconciling the daily financial transactions at the end of each shift. He was present when I opened the envelope, present when I corrected the error, present when I placed the correct money order inside and sealed it back up. We photocopied everything. We documented everything. My supervisor at the time was also present and aware.

The customer had paid for a fifty dollar money order. I had imprinted five hundred dollars. The error was caught, documented, corrected, and witnessed. Nothing was stolen. Nothing was missing. The customer received exactly what they paid for.

The Post Office sent me home anyway. The charge was failing to protect the sanctity of mail.

I went back to Temple University. Again.

A year later, the hearing concluded exactly as it should have: no wrongdoing found. The Post Office acknowledged that its own process created conditions where clerks like me could not resolve such errors without essentially incriminating themselves, and that the system needed examination. A second year's salary came back to me as a lump sum. All benefits restored.

Two attempts. Two years of my life interrupted. Two lump sum settlements. And a resolve that had become, if anything, harder and more certain than it had been before.

I was not going anywhere.

THE CLIMB

By the time I became a full-time supervisor the path had been longer and more complicated than most people's. It had included a car accident and a hostile manager and two wrongful attempts at removal and two return trips to Temple University and two lump sum settlements and more union grievances than I could easily count.

What it had also included was Gregory Turner.

Mr. Turner was the manager at Richmond Station in Philadelphia who promoted me from acting supervisor to a permanent position. He was another one of those people who understood that what a person has been through is not the same as who a person is. We are still friends today. The ones worth keeping tend to stay.

From Richmond I moved through several more stations in Philadelphia in acting manager roles. There was an area manager during this period who used me regularly in those acting capacities, assigning me to offices where he needed someone capable and trusted to hold things together. But when I applied for permanent positions at those same offices, he would not promote me.

I asked him about it directly. I am not the kind of person who lets that kind of question sit unanswered.

He told me the truth, which I will give him credit for even though the truth was disqualifying. He said he was afraid that promoting me would one day result in me becoming his boss. He did not want that.

I thought about that for a long time. The fear of someone's potential as a reason to suppress it. The choice to keep a capable person small so that she would not outgrow the space you were comfortable with her occupying. I have seen that particular brand of small-mindedness in every institution I have ever worked in, and it never stops being what it is: a person's insecurity dressed up as a management decision.

Area Manager Kim Floyd had no such insecurity. Ms. Floyd promoted me to manager of Market Square Post Office in Philadelphia and in doing so opened the door to everything that came next.

> ***Every door that closed in front of me was eventually opened by someone who was not afraid of what I might become on the other side of it.***

THE LESSON

Thirty-eight years in any institution will teach you things that cannot be taught any other way.

Here is what the Postal Service taught me that I carry into every room I enter today:

Systems are only as good as the people willing to hold them accountable. The contract matters. The process matters. But when a manager decides to weaponize either of those things against a person they want to remove, the system requires someone who knows it well enough to fight back. I was that person for myself. I tried to be that person for others.

People will show you who they are through their fear. The manager who would not promote me told me more about himself in that honest moment than he had in years of working together. Fear of someone else's potential is a confession. It tells you exactly what they think you are capable of, which is usually more than they are willing to say out loud.

And this: the right mentor at the right moment changes everything. Eric Coleman who set aside the file. Gregory Turner who said yes when others had said not yet. Kim Floyd who opened a door. None of them had to do what they did. They did it because they were the kind of leaders who looked at people and saw what was there rather than what others had decided to see.

I have tried to be that kind of leader. I have not always succeeded. But I have always tried.

The Post Office gave me thirty-eight years. I gave it everything I had. That is not loyalty. That is mastery. And mastery, unlike loyalty, belongs to you when it is over.

> ***Loyalty is what you give an institution. Mastery is what you keep when you leave it.***

The Postmaster

I want to tell you about the shoes first.

I used to say this to my daughter Victoria when she was in school and the conversation turned to finishing her degree. I would ask her: have you ever gone to Macy's, bought a pair of shoes, paid for them at the register, and then left them sitting on the counter and walked out of the store?

She would say no.

I would say: a college degree is the same thing. You do not leave anything on the counter that you have to pay for.

I say that now because in November 2004, after years of starting and stopping and returning to classrooms during car accidents and attempted wrongful terminations and the full-time work of raising two children and managing a Post Office, I finally picked up my shoes.

My degree is from the University of Phoenix. Bachelor of Science in Business Management. Conferred on the thirtieth day of November in the year two thousand and four, to Kim Willis.

It is not the forensic pathology degree I once planned. It is not the biochemistry major I declared at Temple University in 1986 and then again and then again. Life redirected the dream without canceling it, the way life tends to do when it has other plans for you that you cannot yet see. What I ended up with was a degree in the field I had actually been practicing for years: management. Systems. People. The business of keeping things running when everything around you is conspiring to make that difficult.

I finished my degree because my son graduated high school in 2003. My daughter was set to graduate in 2009. I was asking them to go to college, to get their paper, to not leave their shoes on the counter. I could not do that credibly without doing it myself. Part of that degree was paid for by military benefits I had earned as a disabled veteran after receiving a medical discharge. Part of it came out of my own pocket. All of it was mine to finish.

I am a college graduate. I want that in the record.

> ***You get no credit for being a college student. The credit goes to the college graduate. I am one.***

BOSS LADY

The name came from Philadelphia.

Not from a title. Not from a certificate. Not from anything the Postal Service gave me. My carriers gave it to me, the men and women who worked under my supervision in Philadelphia, who decided at some point that I had earned something that no job description could fully capture.

Boss. Boss Lady.

I will be honest: I was not immediately comfortable with it. Something about being called Boss felt presumptuous, like claiming credit for an authority I was still learning how to hold. I had spent years as the person who showed up for everyone else, the union steward, the acting supervisor, the one who stepped in and stepped up and stepped forward on behalf of people who needed someone to go first. Being called Boss felt like a different posture than the one I had always occupied.

But I watched how they said it. I listened to what was underneath it. And over time I understood that Boss Lady was not a challenge or a complaint. It was an acknowledgment. It was those employees telling me: we see what you are doing, we know what it costs, and we respect it.

That name followed me south. It arrived in Georgia before I did, in the sense that the kind of leader who earns a name like that does not leave it behind when she crosses state lines. You either are that or you are not. I was.

I have been Boss Lady from Philadelphia to Roswell to Jacksonville to Thomson. The Postal Service gave me titles. My people gave me my name.

> ***Titles come from institutions. Names come from people. The names are the ones that last.***

WHAT NOBODY TELLS YOU ABOUT BEING A POSTMASTER

I never planned to be a Postmaster.

I knew I would rise. I had always known that. My father had planted that particular seed in me before I could articulate it, telling me from the time I was a little girl reaching for the nursing profession that I should not be a nurse. I should be a doctor. Do not stop at the supporting role when the top role is available to you. Aim for the thing itself.

I watched Dr. Quincy, M.D. on television and decided that forensic pathology was going to be my life. That did not happen. But what happened instead, across thirty-eight years of Postal Service, was the same essential lesson in a different uniform: whatever you do, be the best version of it. Do not settle for the floor of a room you could run.

I became a manager. I had worked various stations as an acting manager and permanent manager, had done the detail to San Francisco, had led teams in Philadelphia, Florida and eventually in Georgia. But when the opportunity came to apply for the postmaster position in Thomson, Georgia, something felt different about it.

Being named manager and being named Postmaster are technically comparable in level and compensation. The distinction is largely in the title. But the title carries history. To become a Postmaster is to join a line of people who held that position in that specific community, in that specific place, responsible for the mail of everyone who lives there. It is a public trust in the most literal sense of the word.

I wanted it. And when the certificate arrived with the name Kim A. Willis printed on it, below the words Postmaster, Thomson, Georgia, effective July 20, 2019, I felt something I had not expected to feel.

I felt my father.

Ernest Preston Willis, who never got to meet his grandson, who never crossed the threshold with his arms full of gifts, who taught me without knowing he was teaching me that you do not settle for supporting roles in your own life. I carried him to that Post Office in Thomson, Georgia the same way I have carried him to every room I have ever walked into that required me to be more than I thought I was ready to be.

> ***I became a Postmaster in a small Georgia town and felt my father's pride from thirty-four years away. Some lessons take a lifetime to receive.***

HER SIGNATURE

When the certificate arrived I looked at the signature first.

I had hoped, quietly and specifically, that it would be hers. Megan Brennan had become the 74th Postmaster General of the United States in 2015, the first woman to hold that position in the institution's entire history. She led the Postal Service until 2020. My appointment as Postmaster of Thomson, Georgia was effective July 20, 2019, which placed it squarely within her tenure.

Her name and her signature are on my certificate.

I want to be clear about why that mattered to me. For the vast majority of the Postal Service's history, the path to Postmaster General required rising through the ranks of the institution itself. You earned it from the inside over years of demonstrated leadership. Megan Brennan was that kind of leader. She had given her career to the Postal Service, had risen through it the way I had risen through it, and had reached a height that no woman before her had reached.

Her successor was not a product of the Postal Service. He was a businessman appointed from outside. That is a different kind of leader and a different kind of institution, and I will leave my opinion of that transition where it belongs, which is between me and the people who were there.

What I will say is this: the certificate I hold was signed by a woman who earned her way to the top of the same institution I gave thirty-eight years of my life to. When I look at that certificate I do not only see my name. I see what two women, from entirely different backgrounds and paths, accomplished inside the same system.

That is worth naming.

HOW I LED

I learned something early in my management years that I never unlearned: you get what you give.

I had seen the other way. I had worked for managers who led through fear, through distance, through the particular coldness of people who have confused authority with respect. I had watched those managers get the minimum from their people, the exact amount of effort required to avoid consequences and not one ounce more. And I had decided, long before I ever had people reporting to me, that I was never going to be that.

I treated my employees with dignity. Every single one of them. Not because it was policy. Because it cost me nothing and returned everything. A person who feels seen and respected by the person they work for will do things for that leader that no job description requires. They will stay late without being asked. They will cover a gap without being told. They will bring their best on the days when their best is hard to find, because they know that the person they work for notices.

I gave awards. I printed certificates on my own computer and put them in official postal folders and handed them out for attendance, for performance, for the small daily excellences that institutional bureaucracy rarely bothers to acknowledge. I gave gift cards. At my last Post Office in Thomson, where the office was small enough that everyone knew everyone, I made personalized T-shirts for every member of my staff at Christmas. Not just the clerks. The carriers, the custodians, the supervisor.

Everyone who showed up every day to make that office run.

I was told when I first joined the Postal Service that the Post Office does not fire people. People get themselves fired. I carried that with me into every leadership role I held. In thirty-eight years of management, I can think of two people I had terminated. Both were rightfully so. Two people in thirty-eight years. That is not a record I am proud of in a boastful way. It is a record I am proud of because it reflects what I believe about people: most of them, given clarity and dignity and accountability, will do the right thing.

My employees called me Boss Lady. I heard from people who worked for me that if someone did not get along with my decisions, it was probably a them-thing and not a me-thing. I will take that as the highest compliment I ever received in thirty-eight years of Postal Service.

> ***The Post Office will never know every name of every person who kept it running. But those people know who saw them. I made sure they knew I did.***

ROSWELL TO THOMSON

I came to Georgia in 2014.

The decision to leave Philadelphia was not made quickly or lightly. I had been looking toward the end of my career with the kind of clarity that comes when you have spent long enough in one city to know exactly what your future there would look like, and you find yourself wanting something different. I had always known that Philadelphia was not going to be where I finished. I had left it once for the Navy, returned, built a career, and now I was ready to leave again, this time on my own terms and at my own pace.

Georgia made sense. The cost of living. The climate. The ideal retirement location. The sense that there was room to build something new. I applied for a manager position in Roswell, Georgia and earned it. I was presented with an offer only 45 minutes after my interview. The Postal Service relocated me, which was important to me: I was not coming to Georgia at my own expense. I had done enough for the institution over enough years that when I was ready to move, they moved me.

Roswell was not without its complications. There was an area manager above me during my time there whose competence I will not detail and whose name I will not provide, because giving her any more of my pages than this sentence would be more than she deserves. What I will say is that when you find yourself working under someone whose foot is on your neck rather than in your corner, you do not sit still. You network. You look for doors. You stay visible to the people who matter.

I became an acting area manager in Atlanta. I did a detail to the route team in San Francisco, California, another city I had always wanted to know. I came back. I applied to Jacksonville, Florida and was promoted to manager there. I stayed in Jacksonville for a couple of years, coming home to Marietta just once a month, though my daughter Victoria was a flight attendant during that time which meant I could fly for free and I used that benefit without shame or restraint.

And then Thomson came available.

Thomson, Georgia is a small city, the county seat of McDuffie County, about an hour and a half from my home in Marietta. Taking the Postmaster position there was technically a downgrade from my Jacksonville role in terms of office size and scope. I took it anyway. I was ready to be home more consistently. I was ready to leave every Monday morning and return every Friday evening and spend my weekends in the house I had built my Georgia life around. Jacksonville had been worth it. Thomson was better.

I am the first African American woman to serve as Postmaster of Thomson, Georgia.

I want you to sit with that.

Not because I need you to applaud me, though I will not pretend the acknowledgment does not matter. But because I need you to understand what that sentence actually contains. Thomson, Georgia is a small city in McDuffie County, about an hour and a half from my home in Marietta. It is not a major metropolitan market. It is not a place where firsts like this are assumed or expected or easily made. It is a place with a Post Office that has been serving its community for generations, with a list of Postmasters that stretches back further than any of us in that building could fully account for.

I am the 8th officially appointed Postmaster in that office's recorded history.

And I am the first African American woman to hold that position.

I did not grow up knowing that was possible. Not because I lacked ambition, but because the path to that seat was not a path that looked like me. The Postmasters before me were men, and then a woman, but not a woman who looked like me, not a woman who came from where I came from, not a woman who had started on an automation floor making less than nine dollars an hour and been sent home twice by the very institution she was fighting to serve.

I think about the little girl on Willard Street who watched her father build a motorcycle in the basement and decided she could build things too. I think about the eighteen-year-old who walked into the Post Office with a newborn son and a dream she had agreed to defer. I think about every door that closed, every manager who underestimated, every moment I was told in words or in silence that the ceiling was lower for someone like me.

And then I think about that certificate. Kim A. Willis. Postmaster. Thomson, Georgia. Effective July 20, 2019. Signed by Megan Brennan, the first and only female Postmaster General of the United States.

Two women. One institution. History made twice in the same moment.

I have carried a lot of things in my life. I have carried grief and determination and a U-Haul full of everything I owned across 2,700 miles of American highway. I have carried my father's pride and my mother's spine and my brother Troy's memory into every room I have ever walked into.

This one I carry differently. This one I carry out loud.

I am the first African American female Postmaster of Thomson, Georgia. The record says so. History says so. And I say so.

That is confirmed. That is the record. And it is mine.

What I know for certain is what that certificate means. A girl from North Philadelphia, who wanted to be a forensic pathologist, who became a window clerk, who became a union steward, who became a supervisor, who became a manager, who drove a U-Haul across the country and raised two children and earned a degree and kept moving every time something tried to stop her, that girl became the Postmaster of Thomson, Georgia. Effective July 20, 2019. Signed by the first and only female Postmaster General of the United States.

> ***I did not plan to be a Postmaster. I planned to be the best at whatever I did. The Postmaster part took care of itself.***

THE LESSON

There is a version of the Post Office story that sounds like endurance.

Thirty-eight years. Two attempted wrongful removals. A car accident. A few hostile and insecure managers. A system that sometimes worked against the very people who kept it running. Thirty-eight years of showing up anyway.

That version is true. But it is not the whole story.

The whole story includes Eric Coleman setting aside the file. Gregory Turner saying yes. Kim Floyd opening the door. The carriers in Philadelphia who gave me a name. The clerks in Thomson who wore their personalized Christmas T-shirts with something that looked like pride. The degree on my wall. The certificate in my hands. The signature of a woman who proved that the top was reachable.

Here is what thirty-eight years of managing postal operations taught me that I carry into every consulting room I walk into today:

Technology changes faster than institutions do. The automation floor I stood on in 1989 and again in 1991 was a different world from the one I left in 2024. The machines multiplied. The manual processes shrank. The workers who adapted, who learned the new systems, who refused to be left behind by the next wave of change, those workers survived and led. The ones who waited for the institution to train them into the future were often waiting a long time.

People are the system. Every process, every machine, every procedure exists because a person designed it and another person operates it and a third person supervises it. When you treat people well, the system works. When you don't, the machine jams. I had stood at enough jammed machines in my life to know that the jam is almost never about the machine.

And this: the forensic pathologist dream did not die. It transformed. I spent thirty-eight years in service to the public, managing the flow of communication between people, holding institutions accountable, speaking for those who could not speak for themselves. Dr. Quincy, M.D. investigated the truth on behalf of the dead. I investigated the truth on behalf of the living. Different methods. Same instinct.

The dream never dies. It just finds the shape that fits the life you actually have.

> ***Thirty-eight years. Two kids. One degree. One certificate. One name the people gave me that no institution ever could. That is what mastery looks like when you are done counting.***

The Healthcare Years

You have already met Marc.

He arrived after midnight on December 16, 1991, at the same hospital where his cousin Victoria arrived at noon on the same day. My sister Tina's son. The boy born on the other side of twelve hours from my daughter, in the same building, the Willis women doing what they have always done, which is refuse to let the important moments happen separately when they could happen together.

Marc grew up. He built a career in healthcare technology, specifically in the world of Electronic Medical Records, the digital systems that hospitals and clinics use to manage patient information. He is knowledgeable and well regarded in that space. And during my postal career, when I was looking at what came next with the particular hunger of a person who has never been willing to stop learning, I asked him to bring me in.

Take me under your wing, I told him. Teach me what you know.

He did.

I want to pause on that for a moment because it is easy to move past it too quickly. My nephew Marc, born the same day as my daughter, opened a door in his field for his aunt who had spent her entire career in the Postal Service. He shared his knowledge. He shared opportunities when they became available. He trained me in the fundamentals and trusted me to take those fundamentals and build on them. He is well known and respected within the EMR world, and he did not have to do any of what he did for me. He did it because that is who he is and because that is what this family does.

> ***Some people open doors. Some people build them. Marc did both for me and I will not let that go unnamed.***

THE WORK

Electronic Medical Records, or EMR, and the related term Electronic Health Records, EHR, refer to the digital systems that healthcare facilities use to manage patient information. Before these systems existed, medical charts were paper. A doctor wrote notes by hand. A nurse filled out forms. Records lived in physical folders in physical filing cabinets and moved through a facility the same way mail once moved through a post office, manually, slowly, and with significant room for error.

The transition from paper to digital changed everything about how healthcare information moves, and like every significant technology transition, it required people who could teach other people how to use the new system. That is where I came in.

My role as an EMR Analyst and Trainer was to travel to hospitals, clinics, and healthcare facilities across the country and train the people who work there, any person whose job involved touching a patient chart, how to use the electronic system that facility had implemented. I have worked with GE Centricity, Athena, Oracle, Cerner, Meditech, WellSky, and others, including proprietary systems built specifically for individual organizations. Each system has its own logic, its own interface, its own way of organizing information. Each facility has its own workflows, its own culture, its own particular way of doing things that has to be understood and respected even as you are asking people to change it.

When a facility goes live with a new EMR system, which means the day they switch from the old way to the new way, the pressure is intense. Patients are still coming in. Procedures are still happening. The work does not pause for the technology transition. A go-live is exactly what it sounds like: the system is live, the staff has to use it, and someone has to be there to make sure they can.

Many times I have been that someone.

I stood at the front of classrooms full of nurses, physicians, medical assistants, billing staff, intake coordinators, and anyone else whose job brought them into contact with patient information, and I taught them how to navigate a system that many of them had not asked for and some of them actively resented.

> ***Training adults who do not want to be trained is its own advanced degree. I earned that one in the field, not in a classroom.***

NOBODY LIKES CHANGE

Here is the truth about training adults in technology: the technology is almost never the problem.

The problem is change. People build muscle memory around their processes. A nurse who has been charting on paper for twenty years has developed a rhythm, a shorthand, a system that works for her even if it does not work for the institution. Asking her to abandon that and learn something new is not just a technical request. It is a personal one. You are asking her to become a beginner again at something she was expert in, in front of her colleagues, under pressure, with patients waiting.

That is hard. I understood that it was hard because I had lived a version of it every time an institution I worked for changed its systems. I had watched the Post Office automate. I had watched paper processes become machine processes become digital processes. I had been the person at the machine that kept jamming, and I had also been the person who figured out what the new machine was trying to do and made it work anyway.

Some facilities had already transitioned to a major EMR system like Epic and did not want to switch to something new. Some had been on paper so long that the very concept of a digital chart felt threatening. Some staff were cooperative and curious. Others made it clear from the moment I walked in that they intended to outlast this particular initiative the way they had outlasted every previous one.

I did not take it personally. I had been a union steward. I had managed postal facilities where the headcount ran well past forty, and others where it ran well under, every one of them with their own personalities pointed in their own directions. I knew that resistance was not usually about me. It was about the thing being asked, and about the history of being asked things that did not always work out the way they were promised.

What I also knew was this: if I treated the resistance with patience and dignity, if I acknowledged that the previous way had worked and was not being replaced because it was bad but because the new way was better, if

I made the learning feel possible rather than punitive, most people came around. Not all of them. But most.

I trained doctors. Nurses. Clinical staff across some of the most complex care environments in the country. I stood in classrooms and I taught and I answered questions and I stayed late when the go-live hit complications and I came back the next day when people needed a second pass at something they had not caught the first time.

I wanted to be a doctor once. I ended up training them instead.

> ***I told my students often: I wanted to be a doctor. Life had other plans. Now I train them. I call that a promotion.***

THE ROAD

Healthcare IT took me places I would not have gone to on my own.

I have always loved to travel. The Navy sent me to San Diego and I drove home through seven states alone in a U-Haul. The Post Office planted me in Philadelphia, then Georgia, then Florida, and briefly California, building a life one city at a time. But EMR work took me somewhere different, not to live, but to witness. Hospitals and clinics and healthcare facilities in cities and towns across the country, each one its own ecosystem, its own community, its own particular version of the American healthcare experience.

I want to be clear about something: I was able to do this work the way I did it because I was free to. From the time I came to Georgia in 2014, I have been single. I have had relationships. I have had a full and rich personal life. But I have never had a husband, never had someone at home whose needs required me to stay put, never had to negotiate my professional freedom with another person's expectations of my time. The same fear of marriage that cost me Greg, that I have carried since I watched my parents' grief quietly disassemble what they had built together, also gave me something I did not fully understand I was being given: total autonomy over my own life.

I could go wherever the work was. I could stay as long as the engagement required. I could come home when I was done and leave again when the next call came. Some people would hear that and call it lonely. I have never called it that. I have called it freedom. It is the freedom I went looking for the first time I stood at that payphone on the fourth floor of the 30th Street Post Office and decided I was done standing still.

The road is not a consolation prize for people who do not have someone waiting at home. The road is its own kind of life, with its own rewards, its own particular gifts. I have eaten at tables in cities I would never have visited. I have met people in waiting rooms and hotel lobbies and hospital break rooms who became part of my story. I have seen this country from angles that most people who live in it never see, the backstage of its healthcare system, the places where the work of keeping people alive actually happens, at all hours, under impossible pressure, with never enough staff and never quite enough time.

I am grateful for every mile of it.

THE THREE OFFERS

In the fall of 2025, within a single week, I received three separate requests for EMR positions. Each one was a six-figure opportunity. Each one came from an organization that had found my resume and determined I was a strong candidate.

I turned all three down.

I want to sit with that for a moment because it represents something I was not always able to say. There was a time in my life, many times actually, when six figures would have been the answer to a question I did not know how to stop asking. When I was a casual clerk making five dollars an hour with a newborn son and a biochemistry textbook I no longer had time to open. When I was out on medical leave and the Post Office was building a file against me. When I was driving a U-Haul across the country with nothing but paper maps and the stubborn conviction that something better was waiting on the other end of the road.

I am retired. I am financially stable. I have options. And having options means that I get to choose, which means that the work I take on now is work I actually want to do.

I turned down three six-figure offers in a week because I am building Kidovi AI, because I am in a season of my life that I have earned, and because from the time I walked into kindergarten at five years old, somebody else has had a plan for what my days looked like. School. Then more school. Then the Post Office. Then the Navy. Then the Post Office again. Then healthcare IT. Thirty-eight years of someone else's clock.

I set the alarm now. And some mornings I decide not to set it at all.

> ***After thirty-eight years of showing up when the institution said to, I earned the right to show up when I say so. I exercise that right every single day.***

I have always liked to learn new things. That is not a recent development. It is the same instinct that made me change my major three times at Temple University, that made me call the Navy recruiter on a work break without having planned to, that made me ask my nephew Marc to teach me everything he knew about electronic medical records when most people in my position would have been thinking about coasting to retirement.

I keep my mind sharp deliberately. I have watched what happens when people stop challenging themselves, when they decide that what they already know is enough and stop reaching for what they do not know yet. I watched my grandmother go through what they called senility then and call Alzheimer's and dementia now, and I decided very early that I was going to fight that with everything I have, which means I am going to keep learning for as long as I am capable of learning.

Artificial intelligence presented itself at the right moment. Not because it was fashionable, though it certainly became that. But because it was the next hard thing, the next system that required understanding from the ground up, the next wave of change that was going to reshape how organizations operated and how professionals served their clients.

I recognized it immediately. Not as technology I was afraid of. As a problem I already knew how to approach. I had implemented systems in organizations that did not want them. I had trained people who resisted change. I had taken complex institutional processes and broken them down into language that working professionals could absorb and apply. I had done all of that in the Post Office and in healthcare and in the Navy before either of those.

AI was the new EMR. The technology was different. The work was the same.

And there was one more full circle waiting for me in it.

When I graduated from the University of Phoenix in 2004 with my degree in Business Management, I began consulting for businesses. Helping them organize, implement, structure, set up systems that worked. I did that for clients for years, even while the Post Office occupied most of my professional life. Then healthcare IT called and I answered. Now AI is calling and I have answered that too.

But here is what I did not see until I was already inside it: I have been doing this work for twenty years. Helping businesses understand and implement new systems. Helping people navigate technology that felt foreign until it felt natural. The AI consulting I do now through Kidovi AI is the same essential work I have been doing since 2004, built on thirty-eight years of postal operations and a healthcare IT career and a military background and a childhood that taught me that systems break and people bend and the only constant is the person willing to keep showing up.

I did not come to AI as a beginner. I came to it as someone who had been preparing for it her entire career without knowing that is what she was doing.

> ***Every system I ever learned, every room I ever trained, every machine I ever fixed was preparation for this. I just did not have a name for it yet.***

THE LESSON

Here is what this chapter is really about.

It is not about healthcare IT specifically, though healthcare IT was good to me and I was good at it and I carry it with respect. It is about what happens when you commit to being a person who never stops learning.

I wanted to be a forensic pathologist. Life said no. I became a postal worker, a Navy veteran, a union steward, a supervisor, a manager, a Postmaster, an EMR trainer, and an AI consultant instead. At every transition, someone looked at my background and saw something that did not fit the role I was applying for. At every transition, I looked at my background and saw exactly the preparation that role required.

The skills traveled. They always travel. The person who can navigate a ship can navigate a system. The person who can manage a postal facility through a technology transition, and I have managed facilities with well over forty people and some with far fewer, can manage any clinical team through one. The person who has spent a career making complex systems accessible to resistant adults has the exact skill set that the AI era needs most.

You do not need a computer science degree to do meaningful work in artificial intelligence. You need systems thinking. You need communication skills. You need the ability to sit across from a person who is afraid of something and make it feel survivable. You need discipline and curiosity and the willingness to be a beginner again when the next hard thing arrives.

I have been a beginner many times. It has never killed me. It has only ever made me more.

Marc opened the door to healthcare IT. I walked through it. Healthcare IT opened the door to AI. I walked through that one too.

I keep walking.

> ***The title on your business card changes. The person holding the card does not. Expertise is portable. Take it everywhere.***

The Prompt Master

Before I tell you about artificial intelligence I need to tell you about a little girl who spent a lot of time alone in her room.

I was the oldest of five. There was a two year gap between me and Troy, who is gone. Three years between me and Keary, who was a boy and therefore not particularly interested in the things I was interested in. Then Gloria and Tina, the youngest, who had each other. I was the oldest and in many ways the most solitary, not from loneliness but from inclination. I liked my own company. I liked learning things. I liked making things.

I drew. Cartoons mostly. The Flintstones, Holly Hobby, Strawberry Shortcake, whatever was on television, I would sit down and reproduce them freehand, working out the proportions, figuring out how the lines connected, teaching myself to see the way an artist sees. I moved on to people. Profile sketches. Caricatures. I would look at someone and find the essential thing about their face and put it on paper with a particular exaggeration that made it recognizable and funny and true all at once.

Nobody taught me that. I taught myself, in my room, because I was curious and I had time and that is what I did with both.

My father was the same way. Ernest Preston Willis was a jack of all trades in the truest sense of the term. He did not wait for permission to learn things or for someone to teach him. He figured it out. I remember being in the basement of our house at 1925 W. Willard Street, my father and me, building a motorcycle together from scratch. Purple. We built a purple motorcycle in our basement. I was a child holding pieces and handing tools and watching a man make something out of nothing with his hands and his will and his refusal to believe that the thing could not be done.

I think about that motorcycle every time I learn something new. Every time I teach myself a tool or master a process that nobody trained me in, I think about my father in that basement and I wish I could show him what I made. I know he sees it. But I miss being able to hand him the piece and watch his face.

> ***My father built a motorcycle from scratch in our basement. I build AI systems from scratch on my laptop. Different tools. Same instinct. Same blood.***

THE FIRST TOOL

The first AI tool I seriously engaged with was ChatGPT.

That is true for a lot of people. ChatGPT arrived in late 2022 and by early 2023 it was impossible to be online and curious and not encounter it. But the difference between encountering something and actually learning it is the difference between walking past a building and going inside. A lot of people walked past. I went in.

I have always been someone who learns by doing. YouTube University, I call it, because that is genuinely where I have picked up more practical skills than I ever did in any formal classroom setting. I do not wait to be taught. I find the thing, I watch someone who knows it explain it, and then I try it myself until I understand it from the inside.

So I learned to prompt. That sounds simple until you actually do it, at which point you realize that talking to an AI is its own skill, that the quality of what you get out is entirely dependent on the quality of what you put in, and that most people who complain about AI giving them bad results are actually complaining about their own imprecision. I studied prompting the way I had once studied the APWU contract, with the understanding that knowledge is leverage and leverage is power. I learned what the tool could do. I learned where it fell short. I learned the difference between a mediocre prompt and a precise one, and I practiced until precision was my default.

I played in Gemini. I experimented with Flow. I explored the tools that were emerging faster than most people could track them. I was not doing this with a business plan in mind yet. I was doing it because it was new and complex and genuinely fascinating, and because I have never in my life been able to encounter something new and complex and fascinating without wanting to understand it completely.

THE PIVOT

My first projects in AI were creative. I wanted to master the making of AI twins, digital avatars, animated versions of real people placed into films and content. That was what social media was full of at the time and it looked accessible, like something you could learn quickly and use to build an audience and maybe a business.

I tried it. I got good at it. And then I started looking deeper into what AI could actually do, past the surface level content creation that everyone was doing, into the infrastructure underneath. The automation. The business applications. The way that artificial intelligence could be embedded into the operations of a company and fundamentally change how that company functioned.

And I thought about my degree.

I graduated from the University of Phoenix in 2004 with a Bachelor of Science in Business Management. Right out of school I began consulting for businesses, helping them organize and structure and implement systems. I did that work alongside the Post Office for years, because my benefits at the Postal Service were too strong to leave for anything the outside world was offering at the time, but I was doing it. I was always doing it.

The question that crystallized everything for me was this: who has the money, and what do they need from AI?

The answer was not content creators making AI twins. The answer was established businesses, the law firms and medical practices and contractors and service companies that had been operating for years without AI, that did not understand what AI could do for them, that were either afraid of it or dismissive of it or simply unaware that it was already reshaping their industries. Those businesses had budgets. Those businesses had genuine operational problems that AI could solve. And those businesses needed someone who could speak their language, understand their workflows, and implement solutions they could actually use.

That was the work I had been doing for twenty years. I just had not been doing it with AI yet.

> ***The pivot was not from something I knew to something I did not. It was from something I knew to the newest version of it. That is not a leap. That is a step.***

THE PAPER

I earned my AI Consultant Certification on February 24, 2026, through AI InnoVision, accredited by the International Association of AI Consultants and the CPD Standards Office.

I want to be transparent about something. The AI consulting field is new enough that the certification landscape is still developing. There is no single governing body, no universal standard, the way there might be in law or medicine or accounting. What certifications do in a field like this one is demonstrate commitment. They demonstrate that you went beyond self-teaching, that you engaged with a structured curriculum, that you completed the work and earned the credential.

I have always gotten the paper. You do not leave your shoes on the counter after you have paid for them. I paid for this certification, I completed the coursework, and I have it. It sits alongside my degree from the University of

Phoenix and my Postmaster certificate signed by Megan Brennan as evidence of a woman who does not start things she does not intend to finish.

But I want to be honest with my reader: the certification is the beginning, not the destination. The real credential in AI consulting is the work. It is the client whose problem you solved. It is the system you built that actually runs. It is the business that was afraid of AI before you walked in and is using it confidently after you walk out.

I have that credential too. I am building it every day.

K I D O V I

The name of my company is Kidovi AI.

KI. DO. VI.

Kim. Dominic. Victoria.

I have been building businesses under the Kidovi name for years, long before AI entered the picture. My very first independent business was called Kidovi Professional Services. A dog who was part of our family carried that name as well. It is the name I return to when I am building something that matters, because it encodes the reason I build anything at all.

I did not go into business for myself in the abstract. I did not decide to become an entrepreneur because it sounded good or because retirement offered me nothing else to do. I built Kidovi AI because I wanted to create something that bore the names of the people I have done everything for since September 19, 1985, when a boy named Dominic arrived and changed the entire direction of my life, and December 16, 1991, when a girl named Victoria arrived and confirmed that direction was exactly right.

I also wear the name, and no, I do not have any tattoos. I have a cartouche, a large 18-karat gold Egyptian hieroglyphic pendant with the name Kidovi on it. It was a gift, and the story behind it is worth telling. An employee of mine named George Pallathu, originally from India, asked me what I wanted him to bring back from a trip home. I told him something small, maybe a half inch by an inch and a half. What George came back with was well over an inch by three inches, solid 18-karat gold, and more beautiful than anything I would have thought to ask for. I have worn it for close to twenty years. Every time I put it on I think of the kind of person who listens carefully enough to give you something better than what you asked for. The cartouche is an ancient Egyptian symbol, an oval enclosure that surrounds and protects a royal name. The connection to my West African heritage, to an ancestral aesthetic that has always felt like home to me, was not accidental. I wear my family name in a form that connects it to something older and deeper than any business card could express. George made that possible. I have never forgotten it.

Kidovi is not a brand. It is a declaration.

> ***Every system I build carries my children's names. Every client I serve is building something that lasts. That connection is the point of all of it.***

WHY I WAS NOT AFRAID

People ask me sometimes whether I was intimidated by AI. Whether the technology felt overwhelming, whether I worried that it was too late to learn it, whether I thought it was something for younger people or people with technical backgrounds.

The honest answer is no. And not because I am exceptionally brave or exceptionally smart. Because I recognized it.

AI is a system. It has inputs and outputs and rules that govern how it behaves, and the quality of what you get from it depends entirely on how well you understand those rules and how precisely you work within them. I have been working with systems my whole life. The Post Office is a system. The Navy is a system. An EMR implementation is a system. A go-live is a system. Even a union grievance is a system, with its own procedures and timelines and standards of evidence.

I have spent decades standing at the front of rooms full of people who did not want to change, teaching them that the new system was not their enemy. That what it asked of them was not unreasonable. That the discomfort of learning something new was temporary and the benefit on the other side was real. I have done that in hospitals and post offices and naval facilities and city stations from Philadelphia to San Francisco.

Now I do it for businesses that are standing at the edge of the AI era looking in, not sure whether to step forward. I am the person who walks up beside them and says: I have been here before. The system is learnable. The fear is temporary. Come on in.

That is not a new skill. That is the oldest skill I have. It just found a new application.

From Quartermaster to Postmaster to Prompt Master. The tools changed every time. The navigator did not.

> ***I did not come to AI as a beginner. I came to it as someone who had***

been navigating systems her entire life and finally found one that could navigate back.

THE LESSON

Here is what I want every reader to take from this chapter:

The thing you are afraid of is probably not as foreign as it feels. Most of the time, when we encounter something new that intimidates us, what we are actually encountering is a new language for something we already know. AI feels like a different world until you realize it is the same world you have been operating in, with better tools.

You do not need to be young to learn it. You do not need a computer science degree. You do not need to have grown up with technology. You need curiosity. You need discipline. You need the willingness to be a beginner again, which is uncomfortable and temporary and absolutely worth it.

I am fifty-eight years old. I learned to prompt AI the same way I learned to navigate a ship, the same way I learned to run a Post Office, the same way I learned to implement an EMR system in a hospital that did not want one. I sat down with it. I paid attention. I practiced until the unfamiliar became familiar.

You can do the same thing. I promise you that you can.

The girl who drew Flintstones cartoons alone in her room grew up to build AI automation systems for businesses that did not know they needed them. The same instinct, the same hunger, the same refusal to encounter something interesting without learning it completely.

That instinct does not expire. It does not have an age limit. It does not require anyone's permission.

It just requires you to sit down and begin.

> ***The Prompt Master was always in there. She just needed the right prompt to come out.***

The Next Level

I want to be precise about something before I tell you about the first Kidovi AI dollar.

Kidovi AI did not start in 2024. Kidovi started in 2004.

The business was called Kidovi Professional Services Incorporated then. I had just graduated from the University of Phoenix with my Bachelor of Science in Business Management, and I did not let the ink dry before I put that degree to work. My first client was a Philadelphia restaurant called Bottom of the Sea, a popular spot at the time, and what I did for them was everything. I built their website, developed their pricing structures, designed their menus, and wrote their business and marketing plans. I handled the marketing side of their business end to end, because a restaurant that good deserved to be known, and someone had to make sure it was.

Bottom of the Sea is no longer in business. But Kidovi Professional Services was just getting started.

Over the next twenty years, while the Post Office anchored my livelihood and healthcare IT expanded my reach, I never stopped consulting. I worked with dozens of businesses along the way, not always formally, not always under contract, because the Post Office was my full-time commitment and I was not out actively chasing a client roster. But when someone needed help, I helped. I assisted businesses with structure, with startup strategy, with growth and development plans. I helped people think through what they were building before they built it. And as AI emerged I began weaving those tools into my consultations too, showing business owners what was possible before most of them even knew to ask the question.

So when people look at Kidovi AI and call it a retirement project, I smile. It is not a retirement project. It is a twenty-year-old business with a new name, new tools, and no more reason to play small.

> ***"I am not new to this. I grew to this."***

People who are considering starting a business, especially a consulting business, often ask what the hardest part is. They expect me to say getting the first client. They expect a story about rejection and persistence and finally breaking through. That is a satisfying story and it is also not my story.

Getting a client across the line has not been the difficult part for me. When you are knowledgeable, genuinely knowledgeable, and when you can articulate clearly what you offer and why it solves the specific problem the person in front of you is having, the conversation moves naturally. You are not selling them something they do not need. You are showing them something they have already been looking for. That is not hard. That is a conversation. And after twenty years of having that conversation, I know exactly how it goes.

The difficult part, the part I will be honest about, was content. Consistency. Showing up in the digital space with the regularity that builds what marketers call know, like, and trust. The sequence that turns a stranger into a follower, a follower into a lead, and a lead into a client. I had the knowledge. I had the skill. I had the offer. What I wrestled with was the discipline of putting it out there every single day, of being visible and vocal and present even on the days when that felt like the last thing I wanted to do.

I tell you that because this book is built on honesty and because I think it is the part that most people in my position actually struggle with. Not the expertise. Not the delivery. The showing up before anyone is watching, before the audience is built, before the results give you something easy to point to.

That is the real work of scaling a business into its next chapter. And it is the work I was doing even when the first Kidovi AI dollar had not yet arrived.

> ***The hardest part of scaling Kidovi into its AI era was not getting clients. It was showing up consistently before the new clients arrived. That discipline is its own kind of proof.***

THE TRAINING

The first money I made through Kidovi AI came from training.

I put together a bootcamp, a structured session designed to teach individuals and small business owners the essential AI tools that could change how they operated, how they marketed, how they generated content, how they served their clients. Not the advanced technical infrastructure. The accessible, immediately applicable tools that someone could learn in a session, go home with, and start using that same week.

The focus was prompting, which I had come to understand as the fundamental skill of the AI era. Most people interact with AI the way most people interact with a new piece of equipment: they press a few buttons, get results that do not match their expectations, and conclude that the equipment does not work. What I taught was that the equipment works exactly as designed. The variable is the operator. A precise prompt produces a precise result.

An imprecise prompt produces noise. Learning the difference is learnable, and I could teach it.

I walked people through tools they could replicate on their own. I showed them how to turn AI into a content engine, a research assistant, a client communication system, a business development tool. I gave them frameworks and templates and the confidence that comes from watching something work in real time in front of you.

They paid for that. People paid me for that knowledge, which meant the knowledge had value, which meant Kidovi AI was real.

That first payment was not a large number. I am not going to pretend it was. But the size of the first dollar has never been the point. The point is that someone decided what I knew was worth paying for. That is the validation no business plan can give you and no mentor can substitute for. The market told me I had something. I listened.

> ***The first dollar is never about the amount. It is about the proof. Someone looked at what you built and decided it was worth something. Everything else is scale.***

The second thing I did was turn those training sessions into products.

A live bootcamp is a one-time event. You deliver it, people attend, they get value, and then it is over. That is a service. What I wanted was an asset, something that could generate revenue without requiring my presence every time.

The replay model solved that. I recorded the sessions and made them available for purchase at a price point that made them accessible to people who had missed the live event or who wanted to revisit the material on their own schedule. The session happened once. The revenue from it kept coming.

That is the principle that separates a job from a business. A job pays you for your time. A business pays you for the value you create, whether or not you are in the room when it is being delivered. I had spent thirty-eight years trading time for money at the Post Office. I understood the difference viscerally. Building products that could work without me was not just a smart business decision. It was a deliberate departure from the only model I had ever operated inside.

I was building something that could scale. That could reach people I had never met in cities I had never visited. That could teach someone in a different time zone how to prompt an AI tool while I was doing something else entirely.

That felt like freedom in a way that even retirement had not fully delivered yet.

If you are reading this and want to experience that training for yourself, the replays are still available. You can find them at aipromptsandprofits.com. The session happened once. The knowledge does not expire. You will learn something. That I can promise you.

SAMANTHA

While the training business was taking shape I was also building on the service side of Kidovi AI, specifically in the area of AI voice technology.

I built a voice AI receptionist. Her name is Samantha.

Samantha is an AI-powered voice agent designed to answer incoming calls for a business, greet callers professionally, understand what they are calling about, assess their needs, qualify them as potential clients, schedule consultations, and collect their contact information. She does this around the clock, without sick days, without bad days, without the gap that happens when a human receptionist steps away from the desk or a small business owner misses a call because they are already with another client.

Building Samantha taught me something I had suspected but not yet proven: the need for this technology is enormous and most businesses do not know it yet.

Think about how many times you have called a business and reached a voicemail. Think about how many times you have left that voicemail and never heard back. Think about how many times you gave up and called someone else. Every one of those moments is a lost client. Every lost client is lost revenue. For a law firm, a medical practice, a contractor, a consultant, the cost of a missed first call is not just the inconvenience. It is the entire lifetime value of that client relationship, which for some businesses can run into tens of thousands of dollars.

Samantha does not miss calls. Samantha does not put people on hold indefinitely. Samantha does not have an off day. She is available, professional, and consistent in a way that human receptionists, through no fault of their own, simply cannot always be.

When I explain that to a business owner, I do not have to convince them they have a problem. They already know they have the problem. I just show them that there is a solution they had not considered and that I can build it for them.

> ***Businesses are not losing clients because they have bad products. They are losing them because nobody answered the phone. Samantha answers the phone.***

WHAT THEY NEED VS. WHAT THEY THINK THEY NEED

Here is what I have learned from talking to business owners about AI:

Most of them think AI is for tech companies. They think it requires a development team, a significant budget, and a level of technical sophistication that they do not have and do not plan to acquire. They have heard the hype and concluded that it is not for them. They are wrong, but they are wrong in a reasonable way, because nobody has sat down with them and shown them what AI actually looks like inside a business like theirs.

What they need is not a technology lecture. What they need is to see their own problem solved. A law firm does not need a presentation about machine learning. They need to understand that when a potential client calls at nine o'clock on a Saturday morning, which is exactly when people decide they need a lawyer, someone needs to answer that call and handle it professionally. They need to see Samantha in action and realize that the technology already exists and is already deployable and the only question is whether they want it.

That is the gap I fill. Not the gap between ignorance and knowledge. The gap between knowing AI exists and understanding what it can specifically do for the specific business standing in front of me.

I spent thirty-eight years in the Postal Service learning that the most powerful thing a leader can do is make the complex feel manageable. I spent years in healthcare IT learning that the most resistant adult in a training room will come around when they see the technology solve a real problem in real time. I bring both of those lessons into every AI consultation I do.

The first proof of Kidovi AI was not a single transformative client engagement. It was the accumulation of smaller proofs. The training attendee who came back to say the tools changed how she ran her business. The replay purchaser who watched the session twice and then implemented what she learned. The conversation with a business owner where I could see the moment the resistance shifted into possibility.

That is what proof looks like at the beginning. Not a headline. A collection of moments that add up to confidence.

THE LESSON

I want to speak directly to anyone reading this who is standing at the beginning of something.

You will not have all the proof you need before you start. That is the nature of starting. The proof comes from starting, not before it. You build credibility by doing the work, by showing up, by delivering value, by letting the results speak for themselves over time. There is no shortcut to that sequence and no substitute for it.

What I had when I launched Kidovi AI was knowledge, discipline, and a track record from three careers and twenty years of consulting that had everything to do with the skills this work requires. I did not wait until the market validated me. I showed up and let the market meet me.

The Kidovi AI dollars now come from training, replays, voice AI implementations, marketing automation and consulting. And somewhere in that progression, Kidovi AI stops being something I am building and becomes something that is built, something with momentum of its own, something my family's name can anchor for years after I am the one doing the work.

That is the plan. That is always been the plan. I just needed the first dollar to prove it was possible.

It was possible.

It is.

> ***You do not need all the proof before you begin. You need enough proof to take the next step. The rest builds as you move.***

The Blueprint

I want to be precise about something from the beginning of this chapter.

What I am building with Kidovi AI is not a gamble. It is not a retirement hobby that turned into a side hustle. It is not a trend I jumped on because everyone else was jumping. It is a business built on a foundation that took fifty-eight years to lay, and every brick of that foundation was placed by one of the careers, choices, challenges, and lessons that you have read about in the chapters before this one.

A gamble is when you put something at risk without a basis for believing it will work. What I have is the opposite of that. I have three careers of documented results. I have thirty-eight years of operational leadership inside one of the largest institutions in the United States government. I have a military background that taught me discipline and systems thinking before I knew what either of those terms meant. I have a healthcare IT career that took me into the most complex professional environments in the country and asked me to make technology accessible to the most resistant adult learners I have ever encountered.

I have a degree in business management. I have a certification in AI consulting. I have been doing consulting work since 2004, before most of the people currently calling themselves AI consultants had any reason to think about artificial intelligence at all.

This is not a gamble. This is a blueprint. And the blueprint was drawn over the course of an entire life.

> ***You cannot build on nothing. I built on everything. That is the difference between a gamble and a plan.***

WHAT KIDOVI AI ACTUALLY OFFERS

When a client hires me through Kidovi AI they are not hiring someone who learned about AI last year and built a website. They are hiring someone who has spent a career inside the kinds of organizations they are trying to serve.

I have never had a small employer. Every institution I worked for existed before I was born and will exist after I am gone. The United States Postal Service. The United States Navy. The hospitals and healthcare facilities I served across this country. These are not startups. These are centuries-old institutions with complex operations, deeply entrenched cultures, and enormous resistance to change. I learned to work inside all of them, to lead within them, to navigate their bureaucracies, to implement new systems over the objection of people who had been doing things the old way for decades.

That experience is not incidental to what I do. It is the core of what I do. When I sit across from a small business owner who is afraid of AI, who thinks it is not for someone like them, who is not sure the investment is worth it, I am not guessing at what they need. I have spent a career making complex systems accessible to people who did not think they could learn them. I know exactly what that conversation requires.

What Kidovi AI offers, at its foundation, is three things. AI voice systems that answer calls, qualify clients, and book appointments so businesses stop losing revenue every time nobody picks up the phone. AI marketing automation that generates leads, nurtures relationships, and keeps a business visible without requiring the owner to be personally present in the process every day. And AI business consulting that assesses where a company is, identifies where AI can specifically and measurably improve operations, and builds a roadmap for getting there.

Those three offerings exist because I have watched businesses fail at all three of those things. I have been the customer who called and got voicemail. I have been the prospect who was never followed up with. I have been the person in the room when a consultant presented a strategy so disconnected from operational reality that it was useless from the moment it was delivered. I know what is broken because I have seen it broken from every angle.

> ***I do not offer AI solutions because I learned about AI. I offer them because I have spent a career watching businesses fail at the exact problems AI solves.***

GETTING IN THE ROOM

Building Kidovi AI has not been a solitary endeavor.

The community I found through Alicia Lyttle's AI Business Power Circle gave me something I did not know I needed at this stage: peers who were as serious as I was. Alicia and her team lead that community the way the best commanders lead their units, from the front, with information, with accountability, and with the unshakeable conviction that no one gets left behind. I earned my Certified AI Consultant credential through her program, and I am actively enrolled in her Power Circle mentorship program, a certification I am committed to completing. She did not just open a door to this space. She made sure the door stayed open long enough for everyone in the room to walk through it.

Being in those rooms is not for the faint of heart. There is a price of admission, financial and otherwise. You have to show up prepared. You have to contribute, not just consume. You have to be willing to be the person in the room who does not know something and say so, and then go learn it, and come back knowing it. That is the posture these environments require and reward.

I am committed. I am financially invested. I am seeking high returns, not because I need them to survive but because I have earned the right to expect them. I did not spend thirty-eight years building operational excellence to settle for mediocre results in the next chapter of my career.

What being in those rooms taught me that I could not have learned alone is this: the people who succeed in this space are not necessarily the most technically sophisticated. They are the most consistent. The most clear about what they offer. The most willing to do the unglamorous work of showing up every day, building relationships, delivering value before they ask for anything in return. Technical skill is learnable. Consistency and character are earned over time. I came into this space with decades of both.

I also learned where to put my energy and where not to. Some of the most important wisdom I carry going forward came from understanding the difference between mentors who are genuinely invested in your success and people who simply did not offer to help you. Chase the ones who raised their hand. Stop standing at the door of the ones who did not. Your time is your most finite resource and it deserves to be spent with people who mean it when they say they want to see you win.

> ***Surround yourself with people who are for you. Stop chasing people who never offered to be. That distinction will save you more time than any strategy ever could.***

WHY NOT ME

I am occasionally asked, in various forms and with various levels of politeness, why a retired Postmaster with a Navy background is the right person to build AI systems for small businesses.

My answer is always the same: why not? If not me, then who?

The question assumes that the right background for AI consulting is a technical one. That the credential that matters is a computer science degree, or a Silicon Valley pedigree, or a youth spent coding. That assumption is wrong and increasingly obviously wrong as the AI era matures and the businesses that benefit most from it turn out to be exactly the ones that need a translator, not a programmer.

Small and mid-size businesses do not need someone to build them a language model. They need someone to help them understand which tools exist, which ones apply to their specific situation, how to implement them without disrupting what already works, and how to measure whether the investment is paying off. That is not a technical problem. That is a leadership and communication problem. It is the exact problem I have been solving for my entire career.

Thirty-eight years is commitment. Not sitting somewhere collecting a paycheck. Rising from a temporary casual clerk to a window clerk to a Postmaster. Advocating for workers who could not advocate for themselves. Managing stations and teams and operations across multiple cities and four states. Learning new systems every time the institution changed and teaching everyone else to learn them too.

The Navy did not just give me a rank. It gave me a framework for showing up when the work is hard, for operating in high-pressure environments with limited resources and no room for error, for understanding that the mission matters more than the discomfort of the moment. I raised my right hand and meant it. That posture does not leave you when you take the uniform off.

I bring all of that into every client engagement. Not as a resume line. As a way of operating. As the foundation of why my clients can trust that when I build something for them it will work, and when I say I will deliver something I will deliver it.

> ***My background is not despite my past. It is because of it. Every career I have had was training for this one.***

WHAT I WISH SOMEONE HAD TOLD ME

I do not have many regrets about this path. I want to say that first because it is true and because I think it matters for people who are reading this while standing at their own beginning.

What I have is perspective. Things I know now that would have saved me time and energy if I had understood them earlier. And the most important one is this: sometimes you have to spend money to make money, and the quality of what you spend it on determines whether it was an investment or a loss.

I have spent good money to learn great processes. I have invested in certifications, in communities, in tools, in education. None of that felt like a waste because I was investing in myself, and I have always believed that the return on self-investment is the most reliable return available. The degree that took me years to finish. The certification I pursued after retirement. The mastermind memberships that cost real money and return real knowledge. All of it was worth it.

What I also learned, sometimes the hard way, is that you cannot skip the step of finding the right people to learn from. Some of us waste enormous amounts of time asking for help from people who never offered to give it, wondering why we are not getting what we need from them, growing frustrated and bitter at an outcome that was predictable from the beginning. They never said they would help you. That is information. Receive it and redirect your energy accordingly.

Seek out mentors who are genuinely invested in your success. When someone offers to teach you, to share their knowledge, to open a door, take them up on it fully and immediately. Do not half-commit to people who are fully committed to you. Honor the investment they are making in you by making it in yourself.

That lesson applies to building a business. It applies to everything.

I am not in the business of vague aspirations. I do not traffic in dream versions of success that exist somewhere in the indefinite future. I have a plan and I have a timeline and I have the infrastructure and the skills and the track record to execute it.

By the end of 2026, Kidovi AI will be a six figure brand at minimum. That is not a wish. That is a target with specific work behind it, specific offerings in the market, specific processes being built and refined and deployed every day.

The voice AI service is live and buildable. The marketing automation service is live and buildable. The consulting practice is active. The training and digital product revenue is established. Each of those streams feeds the others, and the combined weight of all of them moving in the same direction is what turns a promising start into a sustainable business.

I have been in enough large institutions to know what it takes to build something that lasts. It takes clarity about what you offer. It takes consistency in how you show up. It takes the willingness to do the work on the days when nobody is watching and the results have not yet arrived. It takes the deep-seated belief that what you are building has value and that the right clients will find you if you put it in front of them with enough regularity and enough conviction.

I have all of that. I have always had all of that. The only thing that has changed is the application.

Kidovi AI is going to the top. Not because I am dreaming about it. Because I am building toward it every single day, with the same discipline I brought to a Navy boat, a postal station, a hospital training room, and every other place I have ever shown up and been asked to do something that mattered. My father did not teach me to do it any other way.

> ***I have never built anything small. I do not intend to start now.***

THE LESSON

Every chapter in this book has ended with a lesson. This one ends with a challenge.

Whatever you are building, whatever career you are in or leaving or dreaming about, I want you to sit down right now and answer one question: what is your blueprint?

Not your vision board. Not your one-day list. Your blueprint. The specific, grounded, honest accounting of what you have already built, what skills you already possess, what experiences have already prepared you for what comes next. Because I promise you that preparation exists. It exists in ways you have not fully named yet and in experiences you have not yet recognized as training.

The Quartermaster knew how to navigate before she knew she would need to navigate a Post Office. The Postmaster knew how to manage systems before she knew those systems would eventually be digital. The EMR Analyst and Trainer knew how to teach people through change before she knew that change would one day come wearing a different kind of screen. The Prompt Master was being prepared every day she showed up for work in an institution that was bigger than her and smarter than her and still could not contain her. Your blueprint is already drawn. You just have to read it.

> ***Stop waiting for permission to build what you already have everything to build. The blueprint is in your hands. It has been the whole time.***

The Stack

Let me address the excuses first.

I have heard them all. I have heard them from nurses who did not want to learn EMR. I have heard them from postal workers who did not want to learn new sorting systems. I have heard them from business owners who do not want to learn AI. The specific technology changes. The excuses do not.

The biggest one, the one I hear most often when it comes to AI specifically, is this: I do not want to put my personal information into a machine I do not understand. I am worried about my privacy. I do not trust what it will do with my data.

I understand where that fear comes from. It comes from a reasonable place, a world where data breaches are real and privacy violations happen and technology companies have not always been trustworthy stewards of personal information. That concern is not irrational.

But here is the truth about that concern as it specifically applies to AI tools: the information most people are afraid to put into ChatGPT is information that is already out there. Your name. Your general situation.

The type of business you run. The problem you are trying to solve. None of that is secret. None of that requires you to input your social security number or your bank account or anything that a reasonable person would consider genuinely sensitive. The prompt you write to ask AI for dinner recipe ideas based on what is in your refrigerator is not a security risk. It is a conversation.

The second excuse is the tech one. I am not a tech person. I do not understand technology. This is not for someone like me.

Children are learning AI in schools right now. These are the same children who no longer use physical textbooks, who no longer learn cursive penmanship, who have grown up with tablets and iPads as their primary learning tools. AI is not a future technology. It is a present one. It is being taught to elementary school students. Fight it as you may, it is not going anywhere.

You do not need to understand how it works under the hood any more than you need to understand how your car's engine works to drive it to the grocery store. You need to understand how to use it. Those are completely different things. And using it requires no technical background whatsoever.

> ***You do not need to understand how the engine works. You need to***

know how to drive. AI is the same. Get in the car.

When I introduce someone to AI for the first time, I do not start with business applications or marketing funnels or automation workflows. I start in their kitchen.

Here is one of the first things I teach: open ChatGPT, which is free. Take a photo of the inside of your refrigerator and another photo of your pantry. Upload both. Then type this prompt: I am unable to go to the market today. Based on what you see in these photos, what can I cook for dinner? Please provide recipes and connect me to YouTube videos that show how to prepare each dish.

Watch what happens.

Within seconds you have a personalized dinner plan built from what you actually have on hand, with step-by-step recipes and video tutorials attached. No searching through seventeen recipe websites. No wading through irrelevant suggestions. Just an answer, specific to your situation, delivered immediately.

That is AI. Not a robot. Not a threat. A tool that responded to your specific question with your specific information and gave you something immediately useful.

I have also shown people how to photograph items they want to sell on Facebook Marketplace or eBay and ask AI to write the listing, suggest the price, and identify the best keywords to attract buyers. I take photos at Home Depot in the lawn and garden section and ask AI how a particular plant or feature would work in my outdoor space. Last year I photographed the front of my house and asked ChatGPT to redesign it, to give me ideas for improving the curb appeal based on what it could see. It gave me a full rendering of suggestions. This year I implemented many of them.

Some people pay landscape companies hundreds of dollars for consultations that produce exactly that kind of rendering. I got mine from the free version of ChatGPT on a Saturday afternoon.

That is the entry point. Not a boardroom. Not a business plan. Your kitchen. Your front porch. Your refrigerator. Start with your actual life and let the tool show you what it can do inside it.

> ***The best way to learn AI is not to study it. It is to use it for something you actually need. Start there and everything else follows.***

THE SYSTEM

Once you have experienced what AI can do in your daily life, the path from curious to capable is actually straightforward. Here is the system I teach.

Step one is prompting. This is the foundational skill and everything else builds on it. A prompt is simply what you type into the AI tool. The quality of your prompt determines the quality of your response. Most people who are disappointed by AI results are using weak prompts, vague instructions, minimal context. The more specific you are, the better the output. Learning to prompt well is not technical. It is communication. It is the same skill you use when you give someone clear directions versus unclear ones. You already know how to communicate. You just need to apply that skill to a new conversation partner.

Step two is knowing your tools. AI tools change and evolve constantly, and that can feel overwhelming if you think you need to keep up with all of them. You do not. You need to identify the tools that are relevant to your specific goals and learn those well. ChatGPT for general tasks and ideation. Specialized tools for video, image creation, voice, automation. The landscape shifts but the principle stays the same: find the tool that solves your specific problem and learn it thoroughly before you chase the next one.

Step three is building your stack. Your stack is the specific combination of tools you use regularly to run your life or your business. It is personal. A content creator's stack looks different from a real estate agent's stack, which looks different from a restaurant owner's stack. Identify what you are trying to accomplish, find the tools that accomplish it, and build a consistent workflow around them. Once your stack is working, it works every day without requiring you to reinvent the process each time.

Step four is creating systems from your stack. A system is a stack that runs on its own. You set it up once and it operates without requiring your constant attention. A social media automation system. An email follow-up sequence. A lead capture workflow. An AI voice receptionist. These are systems, built from tools, powered by prompts, running in the background while you do other things. Building systems is where AI goes from being a cool tool to being a genuine business asset.

Step five is iteration. AI is not a set it and forget it technology. The tools improve. Your needs change. Your understanding deepens. The system you build today will be better in six months if you stay curious, keep learning, and keep refining. The people who succeed long term in this space are the ones who treat AI as a practice, not a project.

> ***Prompt. Tools. Stack. Systems. Iterate. That is the path from AI-curious to AI-capable. It does not***

> ***require a degree. It requires a decision.***

THE FREE LIBRARY

My father used to say something that I have carried my whole life.

He would say that schools make doctors and lawyers, but all of that can be done at the free library. Education, after all, is free. The knowledge exists and has always existed and is available to anyone willing to seek it out. What he was teaching me was that the barrier to learning is rarely the cost of the information. The barrier is the willingness to go get it.

That has never been more true than it is right now, in the age of AI.

ChatGPT has a free version that is genuinely powerful. YouTube has tutorials on every AI tool that exists, produced by people who know the tools well and want to share that knowledge. Community groups, free webinars, open-source resources, introductory courses: the information is available and much of it costs nothing. The investment is not financial. It is attention and time and the willingness to be a beginner.

I am not saying you will never need to spend money to advance. I spent money on my certification. I invest in mastermind communities. There are premium tools and paid courses that deliver genuine value. But the starting point, the place where curiosity becomes capability, does not require a significant financial investment. It requires you to sit down and begin.

My father believed in the free library. I believe in YouTube University. The principle is the same. The knowledge is there. Go get it.

YouTube launched in 2005. My father had been gone for twenty years by then. I think about that sometimes. I think about what Ernest Preston Willis would have done with unlimited free video tutorials at his fingertips. This was a man who built a motorcycle from scratch in our basement. Who built a deck behind his house with his own hands. Who made wrought iron railings, which is not a hobby, it is a trade, and who paid for that trade with five of his ten fingers, three on one hand and two on the other, cut in half by the tools required to do the work. And he kept going. With five fingers that were knubs where fingers used to be, he kept building things.

When I sit down at my laptop and pull up a YouTube tutorial to learn something nobody taught me, I think about my father every single time. He would have consumed that platform the way he consumed everything available to him. He would have been unstoppable. He was already unstoppable without it.

So when I say YouTube University, I say it with reverence. And I say it with a little grief. Because the man who taught me that knowledge is free and available to anyone willing to seek it never got to see just how free and available it became.

> ***The knowledge is free. The tools are free. The only thing standing between you and AI capability is the decision to begin.***

WHAT TO DO WHEN YOU CLOSE THIS BOOK

I do not want you to finish this chapter and feel inspired in a general way that leads to no specific action. Inspiration without action is entertainment. I did not write this book to entertain you.

Here is what I want you to do the moment you close this book.

Open ChatGPT. If you do not have an account, create one. It is free and it takes less than five minutes. Then do something simple. Take a photo of something in your home and ask ChatGPT a question about it. Ask it to help you write an email you have been putting off. Ask it to explain something you have always wondered about. Ask it to give you recipe suggestions. Ask it how to help your plant grow healthier. Ask it anything. Just start the conversation.

What you will discover is that talking to AI is exactly that: a conversation. It responds to what you give it. It follows your lead. It does not require you to know anything technical. It requires you to know what you want and to say it clearly. You already know how to do that.

If you can type, you can use AI. I am not a typist. I have never claimed to be. I make mistakes and autocorrect and sometimes talk to my phone instead of typing because it is faster. None of that stopped me from learning to prompt effectively, from building systems for businesses, from earning a certification in AI consulting, from launching Kidovi AI at fifty-eight years old after thirty-eight years in the Postal Service.

If it was possible for me, with my background and my history and all the stops and starts and detours this life has taken me through, then the question I want to leave with you is the same one I asked in the last chapter.

Why not you?

> ***If you can type, you can prompt. If you can prompt, you can build. If you can build, you can profit. The only prerequisite is beginning.***

The AI era does not belong to the young or the technical or the credentialed.

It belongs to the curious. The disciplined. The willing.

Those qualities do not expire at a certain age. They do not require a degree to develop. They do not belong to any particular demographic or professional background. They belong to anyone who decides, today, that they are going to sit down and begin.

I am fifty-eight years old. I am a 100% disabled Navy veteran, a retired Postmaster, a healthcare IT trainer, and a certified AI consultant. I built all of that one decision at a time, one skill at a time, one door at a time, starting from a block in North Philadelphia where a little girl sat in her room drawing Flintstones cartoons and teaching herself to sketch.

She is still in there. She is still learning. She is not done.

Neither are you.

> ***The AI era belongs to the curious. Are you curious? Then it belongs to you. Go claim it.***

The Next Navigator

This chapter is for you.

Not you in the abstract. You specifically. The next Seaman Recruit standing at MEPS about to raise your right hand for the first time, not entirely sure what you just signed up for. The next casual clerk wondering whether this is really where your life is headed. The next window clerk who is good at the job but knows, somewhere underneath the routine, that the job is not the destination. The next union steward who decided to speak up because nobody else would. The next acting supervisor who got the opportunity because someone saw something worth developing. The next manager who was told they were too much for the room they were in.

The next Postmaster who never imagined that title would follow her name. The next EMR trainer stepping into a hospital training room full of people who did not ask for her and do not plan to make it easy. The next person sitting in front of a laptop at midnight trying to figure out what AI can do and whether any of it applies to a life that looks nothing like Silicon Valley.

The next person standing at a machine that keeps jamming, looking around at the fourth floor of wherever they are, wondering if this is all there is.

It is not. I promise you it is not.

> ***The Quartermaster is not a destination. It is a beginning. Every title in this book started the same way: with someone who did not yet know what they would become.***

WHAT I KNOW ABOUT YOU

I do not know your name. I do not know your city or your background or what brought you to this book. But I know some things about you that I am confident enough to say out loud.

I know that you have already survived something. Not the easy kind of surviving where the obstacle is small and the recovery is quick. The real kind, where something happened that you did not choose and could not control, and you had to figure out how to keep it moving anyway. You know what that feels like from the inside. You know the particular weight of it and the particular relief of getting through it and the particular knowledge it leaves you with that you can reference forever after: I have been here before. I survived it before. I can survive this too.

I know that you have been underestimated. Someone, at some point, looked at where you came from or what you were doing or what you had on paper and concluded that the ceiling for you was lower than it actually is. They were wrong. They are usually wrong about people like us, and the proof is that you are still moving, still learning, still reaching for the next thing even when the last thing tried to convince you to stop.

I know that you have more preparation than you have given yourself credit for. Every job you have worked. Every difficult conversation you have navigated. Every time you had to learn something new because the old way stopped working. Every room you walked into where you were the only one who looked like you or came from where you came from. All of that was training. None of it was wasted. The blueprint is already drawn and it has your name on it.

> ***You have been preparing for what comes next your entire life. You just have not called it that yet.***

WHAT NOBODY TOLD ME THAT I AM TELLING YOU

The path is not straight and that is not a problem.

I wanted to be a forensic pathologist. I became a postal worker. I wanted to see London. The Navy sent me to San Diego. I wanted to go to the Persian Gulf. The migraines said no. I wanted to stay in California. The Post Office said come home. Every one of those redirections felt at the time like a door closing. Every single one of them was actually a door opening to something I could not have reached any other way.

The detours are not failures of navigation. They are the navigation. The Quartermaster's job is not to sail in a straight line. It is to get the ship to its destination by whatever route the conditions require. Sometimes the conditions require going around. Sometimes they require waiting. Sometimes they require trusting a course you cannot fully see yet and staying on it anyway.

The institution will not always treat you fairly. I was sent home from the Navy with a ten percent disability rating when I deserved more, and I spent years fighting that before the record was corrected. I was almost driven out of work twice by a postal system that was supposed to protect me. I was passed over for promotions by a manager who was afraid of what I might become. Every one of those things was real and wrong and none of them stopped me. They slowed me. They hurt. They cost me time and energy and peace of mind that I would have preferred to spend differently. But they did not stop me because I did not let them be the final word on who I was or what I was capable of.

You are going to encounter people who are not for you. Who compile files instead of opportunities. Who suppress instead of develop. Who are too afraid of what you might become to help you get there. I want you to know those people in advance so that when you meet them you are not surprised and you do not confuse their limitations for your own. Their ceiling is not your ceiling. Their fear is not your forecast.

And I want you to know the other kind too. The Eric Colemans who set aside the file. The Gregory Turners who say yes when others say not yet. The Kim Floyds who open doors. The Marcs who share their knowledge because that is what family does. Those people exist. They are in your path right now, some of them, even if you have not recognized them yet. When they appear, receive them fully. Do not half-commit to people who are fully committed to you.

> ***The institution does not define you. The setback does not sentence you. The only verdict that matters is the one you render about yourself.***

THE THROUGH LINE

When I look back at everything in this book, from W. Willard Street to NOSC Point Loma to the automation floor at 30th and Market to Thomson, Georgia to the laptop where I build AI systems for businesses that did not know they needed them, I can see a thread that runs through all of it.

The thread is not any specific skill. It is not any specific title or institution or credential. The thread is a way of showing up. Curious. Prepared. Willing to be a beginner again when the next hard thing arrives. Unwilling to let someone else's assessment of my potential become my operating reality.

I have been a Seaman Recruit. I have been a casual clerk. I have been a window clerk, a union steward, an acting supervisor, a supervisor, an acting manager, a manager, a Postmaster. I have been an EMR trainer in hospitals and healthcare facilities from one coast to the other. I have been a student when the degree felt impossible and a graduate when it was done. I have been a founder at fifty-eight years old in an industry that did not exist when I was forty.

The thread through all of it is the same. I showed up. I learned the thing. I did the work. I moved when it was time to move and stayed when it was time to stay and fought when the fight was worth having and let go when holding on would have cost me more than walking away.

That is not a complicated formula. It is not a system that requires a degree or a certification or a particular background. It is a decision, made fresh every morning, to keep it moving. To keep growing. To keep being the kind of person who walks into a room, learns what the room requires, and delivers it.

You already know how to do that. You have been doing it your whole life. You just may not have called it a strategy yet.

> ***The through line of a life well lived is not the titles you collected. It is the posture you maintained. Show up. Learn the thing. Do the work. Repeat.***

ON AI AND WHAT IT MEANS FOR YOU

I want to speak specifically to anyone reading this who is in the early stages of their career, who is working a job they did not plan to stay in forever, who is looking at the AI era and wondering whether there is a place in it for someone like them.

There is. There absolutely is.

The AI era does not need more people who can build the technology. It needs people who can deploy it, explain it, implement it, and make it work inside real organizations with real humans who have real resistance to change. It needs people who understand operations, who have led teams, who have navigated bureaucracies and managed crises and delivered results under conditions that were not ideal and were never going to be.

That is a postal worker. That is a veteran. That is a nurse, a teacher, a healthcare administrator, a small business owner who has been figuring it out for years without anyone handing them a roadmap. The skills that the AI era needs most are the skills that people like us have been building for decades in places that Silicon Valley has never thought to look.

You do not need to wait until you have a tech background to enter this space. You need to start learning now. Open the tools. Study the prompts. Find your stack. Build your first system. Take the course. Join the community. Get in the room. Invest in yourself the way you have always invested in the institutions you worked for, except this time the return comes back to you.

The machine is not going to jam forever. At some point you pick up the phone. At some point you make the call. At some point you decide that the path you have been on has prepared you for the path you are about to take, and you take it.

What are you waiting for?

Alicia Lyttle, who has mentored me through this AI era, always says that no one gets left behind in the AI revolution. This chapter is my version of that promise. No clerk. No sailor. No Postmaster. No EMR trainer. No one who has spent a career showing up and doing the work gets left behind. Not on my watch and not on hers.

FROM QUARTERMASTER TO PROMPT MASTER

I started this book on a street called Willard in North Philadelphia, eight years old, watching smoke rise from my grandparents' house and learning for the first time that the world could change in a morning.

I am ending it here, fifty years and three careers later after two children and a Navy discharge and a postal career and a college degree and a healthcare IT practice and a gold cartouche around my neck with my family's name spelled out in hieroglyphics, building an AI consulting business at a stage of life when most people are settling in.

I am not settling. I have never settled. I do not intend to start.

My father built a motorcycle in a basement from scratch and taught me that the thing you want to make is made by the person willing to make it. My mother attempted to scale a burning building and taught me that love does not recognize impossibility. My grandfather sat on a porch in my Navy cap and taught me that home is not a place you leave behind. It is a place you carry with you and return to stronger than when you left.

Troy did not get enough time. My father did not get enough time. My mother did not get enough time. I think about that. I think about it every time I am tempted to wait, to hesitate, to tell myself that the next chapter of my life can begin later when things are more settled, when I am more ready, when the conditions are better.

The conditions are never perfect. The time is never ideal. The machine will always find a reason to jam. The only question is whether you pick up the phone on your break and make the call anyway.

I did. Every time. And I am still here, still making calls, still building things, still learning, still moving.

KIM. Keep It Moving.

Now I am passing that forward to you. Whatever your beginning looks like. Whatever machine you are standing at. Whatever door you are not sure you are allowed to walk through. Whatever room you have been told is not for someone like you.

Walk through the door. Pull up a chair. Learn the room. Do the work.

The next Quartermaster is reading this right now.

I know because I was her once.

And look where she ended up.

> ***From Quartermaster to Postmaster to Prompt Master. The tools change. The navigator does not. Now it is your turn to navigate.***

✦

Kim A.A. Willis

Quartermaster. Postmaster. Prompt Master.

Photo Gallery

The photos in this gallery are available to view in full color as a free bonus gift.

Visit kidoviai.com/thebook to see the full color gallery.

Scan to view all 42 photos in full color.

Ernest Preston and Donna Willis. Young, beautiful, and full of life. Everything Kim A.A. Willis would become started right here, in the love between these two people.

On top of the world at Grandmom and Grandpop's house in Germantown. Little Kim and her father Ernie, his smile as wide as his pride. She did not know it yet but she was already being held up by people who believed she could go anywhere.

Before the headaches. Before the heartaches. Before any of it. This is Donna and Ernie Willis just being young and alive and having a good time with relatives. Before the devastation of the fire, the separation, the broken home, they were just two people who loved each other and knew how to have a good time.

Keary and Troy. Two little boys in their Sunday best on what would be their last Easter together. Troy Anthony Willis left this world too soon but he never left this family. He is in every chapter of this book whether his name appears or not. He is in the fire that never went out. He is in the reason Kim kept it moving. He was the first to establish a principle in Kim that says tomorrow is promised to no one so be sure to live for today.

Me and my siblings in North Philadelphia, showing up dressed and ready. Left to right: Kim, Gloria, Tina, and Keary at Our Lady of Holy Souls Catholic School. Elementary school Kim on the far left had no idea what was ahead of her. She showed up anyway.

The porch on Willard Street was where everything began. Gloria and Hebrew Thompson, Mom and Dad, holding court the way they always did. The roots of this story run right through this front porch.

This is where it all began. A young single mother stepping off her shift as a casual clerk at the United States Post Office, coming home to the family house on Willard Street and the most important job she would ever have. Little Dominic was just learning to walk. His mother already knew how to run. She did not know it yet but this moment was the first page of a thirty eight year Postal Service story. Gold hoops. LV bag. Great smile. She had everything she needed.

The steps of 1925 were the gathering place. Left to right top: Gloria and Keary. Center: Tina. Far right: Kim. Bottom: a young Dominic. This was before the Navy, before the Post Office career took off, before any of the titles that would come later. This was just a young postal worker in North Philadelphia sitting on her steps with her people. Some of the best moments in life do not announce themselves. They just happen on a random day on the front steps.

Grandmom was sick but nobody told her grandchildren to stay away. They showed up the way she always showed up for them, fully and without hesitation. Top left to right: Victoria, Dominic, and Grandmom Donna. Bottom left to right: Marc and Tiana. She spoiled every single one of them and they loved every minute of it. That is what Donna Willis did, she made everyone around her feel like the most important person in the room.

This is where the first hat was put on. Seaman Recruit Willis. Boot camp. Kim Willis became Quartermaster Third Class Willis. The girl from North Philadelphia stood in front of the American flag and raised her right hand and meant every word. Whatever was ahead of her she was ready. She always was.

Orlando, Florida. Boot camp. The young woman who signed up thinking she was going to be a data processor is positioned third row down, fourth from the left. She had no idea she would eventually become a Quartermaster. The United States Navy gave her options and she changed her plans. That is how it happens. In these rows of recruits standing at attention is the navigator who did not yet know she could navigate. She was about to find out.

Boot camp was done and Dominic came to celebrate. Kim Willis holding her son tight in Orlando, Florida while her shipmates Ranetha Robinson and Sharmane Sullivan stood beside her in their dress blues. They spent the day at an amusement park like they had not just survived one of the hardest things a person can do. Dominic in his red sneakers had no idea his mother had just become a sailor. She knew. And she held him like she had something to prove and something to protect at the same time.

The Navy took Kim to San Diego and Kim shared it with Dominic and Gloria along with a piece of Tijuana Mexico. Little Dominic in his shades and his tracksuit was not missing a single moment. Aunt Gloria came all the way from Philadelphia to visit and they made the most of every minute. Three tacos for a dollar and a memory that never fades.

The Postal Service chapter was just getting started. Kim A.A. Willis receiving her United States Postal Service Certificate of Completion for Essential Foundations for Supervisors on July 19, 2010. Left to right: Plant Manager Mauldin, Postmaster Kenny, Kim A.A. Willis, and District Manager Gallagher. She walked into that room a postal worker and walked out a promoted, Form 50 supervisor. #IYKYK

The nameplate said Kim Willis before the title caught up. West Market Station, Philadelphia. Kim Willis serving as acting manager, not yet promoted but already running the room. Behind her on the wall are the credentials she earned while working full time and raising her children. University of Phoenix degree. Certificates. Awards. A photo from her supervisor promotion ceremony. She did not wait for permission to be great. She just kept building until the title had no choice but to follow.

Some of the best leadership happens on a Saturday with no suit or fancy clothes. This is the Crosstown Post Office in Roswell, Georgia, the station Kim Willis relocated from Philadelphia to manage. When the last delivery was done they fired up the grill, dealt the cards, turned up the music and just enjoyed each other. No titles. No hierarchy. Just a manager and her crew being human together. This is what it looks like when people actually want to show up for work.

This is what management looks like from the inside. Kim Willis at her desk in Roswell, Georgia, overseeing the work floor behind her. The mail is moving. The operation is running. And the manager has her eye on all of it. This is the quiet version of leadership. No ceremony. No audience. Just a woman doing the work she was built to do.

Kim Willis, Officer in Charge, Norcross, Georgia Post Office. Because if you can handle Roswell, you can handle anything. #IYKYK

This is what a plan looks like before anyone else knows about it. Manager Kim Willis at the Pottsburg Post Office in Jacksonville, Florida, filming a behind the scenes video about an idea she had not yet brought to life. The Veterans Memorial Wall existed in her mind before it existed on that blue wall. This smile is not just confidence. It is a woman who already knows what she is about to do. Watch.

A Postmaster who saw her people. Kim A.A. Willis standing beside the Veterans Memorial Wall she designed, decorated, and built at her Jacksonville, Florida Post Office. Every frame on that wall represents a United States Postal Service employee who served this country in uniform, including two veterans who served in other nations but showed up to serve American communities every day. Kim painted the wall blue, hung the stars, collected every photo, and made sure no veteran under her roof was invisible. Words barely do justice to this moment.

They came. They served. They delivered. The team at the Pottsburg Post Office in Jacksonville, Florida gathered in front of their Veterans Memorial Wall, a wall their Manager Kim Willis built because she believed they deserved to be seen. Employees asked if their families could come in just to see the wall and take a photo in front of their picture on the wall. People came from other Post Offices just to see it. It was more than a wall. It was a declaration. These veterans mattered. Kim A.A. Willis made sure of it.

Real systems. Real results. Real people. Kim Willis did not just manage the Pottsburg Station in Jacksonville, Florida, she coached it. She spent time on the floor with her carriers, walking them through the process, showing them how to do it right. The scanning scores improved. And when they did, they celebrated together the way a real team does. Every carrier in this photo earned that moment. Their manager made sure they knew it.

A manager who believed recognition was not optional. Kim Willis presenting Certificates of Achievement to employees at the Mandarin Post Office in Jacksonville, Florida. She believed that when people did the work they deserved to be seen for it. Every certificate in this photo was earned. Every person holding one knew their manager noticed.

The Best of 2018 Annual Awards at the Mandarin Post Office. Five plus years accident free. These are not just names on a graphic, they are postal workers who showed up every single day, did their jobs with excellence, and earned the right to be recognized. Manager Kim Willis made sure they were.

This is what it looks like when a girl from North Philadelphia becomes the Postmaster of Thomson, Georgia. Kim A. Willis holding her official Postmaster certificate signed by Postmaster General Megan Brennan, effective July 20, 2019. The certificate reads: I hereby authorize and empower Kim A. Willis, Postmaster, Thomson, GA. This certifies my special trust and confidence in your intelligence, diligence, discretion and ability to perform the duties of this office. She earned every single word of that.

United States Post Office. Thomson, Georgia 30824. Postmaster Kim A. Willis standing in front of her office, pointing at the name on the wall with true Postal Pride. She knew when this photo was taken that this could be the last chapter of her Postal Service story. Thirty eight years of service. Casual Clerk. Automation Clerk. Window Clerk. Supervisor. Manager. Postmaster. The girl from North Philadelphia pointed at that wall and said yes. This one is mine.

This is what history looks like on a regular day. Postmaster Kim A. Willis and her team standing in front of the Thomson, Georgia Post Office. The first African American woman to hold this position in Thomson, Georgia did not arrive with fanfare. She arrived with a Form 50, a plan, and a commitment to the people standing beside her. Every person in this photo was part of that chapter. They showed up. So did she.

Thomson Post Office. Christmas 2020. The world was in the middle of a pandemic and Postmaster Kim Willis was making personalized stockings for every single one of her employees. She stuffed them with trinkets, made everyone a mask, and made a custom shirt that she printed that said it all. Thomson Post Office. I Survived 2020. She hung every stocking at every clerk's workstation and carrier case so they would find it when they came in to work on Christmas Eve morning. Because that is what this Postmaster did. She showed up for her people. Every single time. In every single way.

Franklin High running back Dominic Bass sprained his ankle early in the 22-0 playoff loss to Washington. He looks glum despite a sideline visit from his mother.

Franklin High running back Dominic Bass sprained his ankle early in the 22-0 playoff loss to Washington. He looks glum despite a sideline visit from his mother. The Philadelphia Daily News captured this moment but they did not capture the full story. His mother had her own jersey made with his name on her back, "Dominic's Mom, #27." Because that is what Kim Willis does. She shows up. Every time. For everyone, especially her children. And with pom poms. She has always been and continues to be their number one cheerleader.

You can take the family out of Philadelphia but you cannot take Philadelphia out of the family. Kim, Dominic, and Victoria representing the Philadelphia Eagles from Georgia. Dominic is holding Kiwa, the family dog who has since gone on to grace. The jerseys never came off. The roots never moved. Once an Eagles fan always an Eagles fan. Fly Eagles Fly.

The uniforms are gone but the bond never left. Left to right: Tina, Kim, Keary, and Gloria, the same four who stood in a row at Our Lady of Holy Souls, now standing together celebrating Keary's birthday. North Philadelphia made them. Life shaped them. But the children Donna and Ernie created never stopped showing up for each other.

This photo lives on walls. Kim's dining room. Tina's living room. Wherever it hangs it tells the same story. Standing back left to right: Dominic, George, Keary, and Marc. Seated on the sofa left to right: Kim, Tina, and Gloria. On the floor left to right: Aliyah, Tiana, Kayla, and Victoria. Kim sat with the clicker in her hand and captured this moment herself, because that is what navigators do. They make sure nothing important gets missed. This family shows up. Every single time.

Christmas 2021. Dominic, Kim, and Victoria gathered under the tree in matching custom pajamas that Kim designed herself because of course she did. The same woman who made personalized stockings for her entire Post Office staff was not going to let her own family have ordinary Christmas pajamas. Each set custom made with a logo she created. Left to right: Dominic, Kim, Victoria. This is what the navigator looks like when she is off the clock. Still creating. Still showing up. Still making every family moment special.

The Prompt Master was open for business. This is the team behind Kim Willis's very first AI Boot Camp, AI Prompts and Profits. Left to right: Chiffon, Victoria, Kim, Marc, Karen, and Tyesha. A retired Postmaster turned AI educator assembled a team, built a brand, and launched a Boot Camp. The navigator had found her next destination. Replays of the Boot Camp are available for purchase at aipromptsandprofits.com.

The Prompt Master in the room where it happens. Kim Willis with the Queen of AI, Alicia Lyttle, at the AI Fuel Profits mixer in Atlanta, 2026. The woman who certified Kim as an AI Consultant and the woman who earned that certification, standing together at the next level. This is not a student and a teacher anymore. This is two builders in the same room. The navigator had arrived.

Two Philadelphians in the AI era building something bigger than themselves. Kim Willis with Nehemiah Neo Davis, award winning author, serial entrepreneur, philanthropist, and coach, at the AI Fuel Profits mixer in Atlanta, 2026. Neo grew up in West Philadelphia and has dedicated his life to serving others through the Nehemiah Davis Foundation. The City of Philadelphia honored him by renaming the street where he grew up Nehemiah Davis Way. He now coaches and mentors entrepreneurs in Alicia Lyttle's Power Circle community. North Philadelphia met West Philadelphia in Atlanta. The navigator and the philanthropist in the same room. Philly always finds its own.

VIP. Kim Willis at the AI Fueled Profits Summit in Atlanta, 2026, standing next to the man whose voice has launched a million journeys. Les Brown. The greatest motivational speaker of our time. The boy who was written off by a system that could not see his greatness grew up to fill arenas. The girl from North Philadelphia who was told the ceiling was lower than it actually was grew up to become a Postmaster, an AI consultant, and an author. Two people in the same room who never got the memo that they were supposed to quit. The navigator had arrived at the right table.

The navigator raised a navigator. Kim Willis and her daughter Victoria at the AI Fueled Profits Summit in Atlanta, 2026. Victoria is not just watching her mother build in the AI era. She is building her own consulting practice right alongside her. A true Mommy and Me of women in the same room at the same summit with the same fire. Kim has always been Victoria's number one cheerleader. The pom poms never went away. They just got upgraded for the AI era.

The Prompt Master takes her seat. Kim Willis at the AI Business Summit in Charleston, South Carolina, 2026. The same woman who navigated ships, ran Post Offices, and trained healthcare professionals on EMR systems was now learning to navigate the AI era on a national stage. She did not come to watch. She came to work.

This is what it looks like when a navigator finds a new stage. Kim Willis practicing her presentation skills and shooting content at the AI Business Summit in Charleston, South Carolina, 2026. The cameras were rolling. The screens were lit. And the woman from North Philadelphia was right where she was supposed to be.

Behind her are the faces of Platinum members from across the country. In front of them is Kim A.A. Willis, hands folded, focused, ready. The AI Business Summit in Charleston, South Carolina, 2026. This is what the next chapter looks like. Real systems. Real results. Real revenue. KIM. Keep It Moving.

This is the third hat. Kim A.A. Willis standing in front of her Kidovi AI brand backdrop at the AI Business Summit in Charleston, South Carolina, 2026. The MacBook is open. The content is being created. The brand is behind her and the future is in front of her. Quartermaster. Postmaster. Prompt Master. The navigator has always known where she was going. She just needed the right coordinates. She found them. Real systems. Real results. Real revenue. KIM. Keep It Moving. kidoviai.com

You made it this far. That means you earned this.

All 42 photos in this gallery are available to view in full color as a free bonus gift from Kim A.A. Willis.

Visit kidoviai.com/thebook to see the full color gallery.

Scan to view all 42 photos in full color.

No cost. No signup. Just the story behind the story in living color. Thank you for reading.

About the Author

Kim A.A. Willis is a mother, a disabled Navy veteran, a retired United States Postal Service Postmaster, an EMR Trainer and Analyst, a certified AI consultant, and the founder and CEO of Kidovi AI, an artificial intelligence automation consultancy based in Marietta, Georgia.

Kim began her career in January 1986 as a casual clerk with the USPS, earning five dollars an hour and raising a newborn son while attending Temple University full-time. Over the next thirty-eight years she rose from the automation floor to the Postmaster's office, leading postal operations across Pennsylvania, Georgia, Florida, and California. She retired in 2024 as Postmaster of Thomson, Georgia, her appointment certificate signed by Megan Brennan, the first and only female Postmaster General of the United States Postal Service.

In between those two moments, Kim served in the United States Navy as a Quartermaster Third Class, earning her rank by outstanding performance and through competitive examination at Naval Ocean Systems Center Point Loma in San Diego, California. She was honorably discharged on medical grounds in July 1991. She is now a disabled veteran and proud of every day she served.

Kim also built a parallel career in healthcare information technology, working as an EMR Analyst and Trainer in hospitals, clinics, and healthcare facilities across the country. Introduced to the field by her nephew Marc, she implemented electronic medical records systems including Athena, Cerner, Meditech, and WellSky, training healthcare professionals to navigate technology that changed how patient care was delivered and documented.

In 2024, Kim turned her attention to artificial intelligence. She earned her AI Consultant Certification through AI InnoVision in February 2026, accredited by the International Association of AI Consultants and the CPD Standards Office. She launched Kidovi AI to bring practical, deployable AI solutions to small and mid-size businesses that need them most.

Kim holds a Bachelor of Science in Business Management from the University of Phoenix, conferred November 30, 2004. She has been consulting for businesses since graduation, a practice that now finds its fullest expression in the AI era.

She is the mother of Dominic and Victoria, and the proud grandmother figure to three miniature dachshunds, Duchess, Nala and Blondi. She lives in Marietta, Georgia, where she builds AI systems, writes, creates, and keeps it moving.

KIM. Keep It Moving.

Work with Kidovi AI

Real Systems. Real Results. Real Revenue.

If this book left you thinking about what AI could do for your business, that thought is worth acting on.

Kidovi AI works with small and mid-size businesses, law firms, medical practices, contractors, consultants, and service providers who are ready to stop losing clients to missed calls, inconsistent follow-up, and manual processes that AI can handle better, faster, and around the clock.

Here is what Kidovi AI builds:

- AI Voice Receptionist Systems: a custom AI voice agent that answers your calls, qualifies your leads, books appointments, and collects contact information 24 hours a day, 7 days a week. Never miss a client again.
- AI Marketing Automation Systems: automated lead generation, follow-up sequences, and content workflows that keep your business visible and your pipeline moving without requiring your constant attention.
- AI Business Consulting: a structured assessment of your business operations, a clear identification of where AI can create measurable improvement, and a

roadmap for implementing it without disrupting what already works.

Kim also offers training and digital products for individuals and teams who want to learn how to use AI tools effectively, including bootcamps, replay sessions, and the frameworks that turn AI-curious professionals into AI-capable ones.

> ***You do not need a tech background. You need the right guide. That is what Kidovi AI is here to be.***

To learn more, book a consultation, or explore current offerings:

kidoviai.com

Follow the journey:

@kidoviAI | @aipromptsandprofits | @theofficialaijawn

Kidovi AI is built on fifty-eight years of showing up, learning the system, and delivering results. Bring your business. We will bring the blueprint.

The Prompt Master Toolkit

Your Five-Step System from AI-Curious to AI-Capable

This page is a reference. Come back to it whenever you need a reminder of where to start or what comes next.

STEP ONE: PROMPT

The foundational skill. A prompt is what you type into the AI tool. The quality of what you get out depends entirely on the quality of what you put in. Be specific. Provide context. Tell the tool what you want, who it is for, and what format you need it in. Precision is not technical. It is communication. You already know how to communicate. Apply that skill here.

STEP TWO: TOOLS

You do not need to know every AI tool. You need to know the ones that solve your specific problems. Start with ChatGPT for general tasks, ideation, writing, and research. Then identify the specialized tools relevant to your goals: video, image creation, voice, automation, scheduling. Learn each one thoroughly before chasing the next. Depth over breadth, at least at the beginning.

STEP THREE: STACK

Your stack is the specific combination of tools you use regularly. It is personal. A content creator's stack looks different from a contractor's stack. Identify what you are trying to accomplish, find the tools that accomplish it, and build a consistent workflow around them. A working stack does the same job every day without requiring you to reinvent the process each time.

STEP FOUR: SYSTEMS

A system is a stack that runs on its own. You set it up once and it operates without requiring your constant attention. A social media automation system. An email follow-up sequence. A lead capture workflow. An AI voice receptionist. These are systems, built from tools, powered by prompts, running in the background while you focus on other things. This is where AI goes from being useful to being transformative.

STEP FIVE: ITERATE

The tools evolve. Your needs change. Your understanding deepens. The system you build today will be better in six months if you stay curious, keep learning, and keep refining. The people who succeed long term in AI are not the ones who got it right the first time. They are the ones who kept going back to make it better. Treat AI as a practice, not a project.

✦ ✦ ✦

One final reminder before you close this book:

Open ChatGPT. If you do not have an account, create one. It is free and it takes less than five minutes. Then ask it one question about something you actually need help with today. Not someday. Today.

That is the beginning. Everything else builds from there.

> ***If you can type, you can prompt. If you can prompt, you can build. If you can build, you can profit. The only prerequisite is beginning.***

kidoviai.com

✦

From Quartermaster to Postmaster to Prompt Master.

The tools change. The navigator does not.